THIS BOOK
BELONGS TO

....

....

Thank you for Purchasing my book and taking the time to read it from front to back. I am always grateful when a reader chooses my work and I hope you enjoyed it!

With the vast selection available online, I am touched that you chose to be purchasing my work and take valuable time out of your life to read it. My hope is that you feel you made the right decision.

I very much would like to know what you thought of the book. Please take the time to write an honest and informative review on Amazon.com. Your experience and opinions will be of great benefit to me and those readers looking to make an informed choice.

With much thanks.

@COPYRIGHT 2024

The content contained within this book may not be reproduced, duplicated, or transmitted without direct written permission from the author or the publisher. Under no circumstances will any blame or legal responsibility be held against the publisher, or author, for any damages, reparation, or monetary loss due to the information contained within this book. Either directly or indirectly.

Legal Notice:

This book is copyright protected. This book is only for personal use. You cannot amend, distribute, sell, use, quote, or paraphrase any part, or the content within this book, without the consent of the author or publisher.

Disclaimer Notice:

Please note the information contained within this document is for educational and entertainment purposes only. All effort has been executed to present accurate, up-to-date, and reliable, complete information. No warranties of any kind are declared or implied. Readers acknowledge that the author is not engaging in the rendering of legal, financial, medical, or professional advice. The content within this book has been derived from various sources. Please consult a licensed professional before attempting any techniques outlined in this book. By reading this document, the reader agrees that under no circumstances is the author responsible for any losses, direct or indirect, which are incurred as a result of the use of the information contained within this document, including, but not limited to — errors, omissions, or inaccuracies.

Table of Contents

1. There Are Not Enough Hours in the Day	5
2. Stop Admiring the Problem	11
3. Let's Get You Back to Your Work	23
4. Perspective 1 – Effective Teams	27
5. Perspective 2 – Systems Thinking	46
6. Perspective 3 – The Diverse Classroom	63
7. Perspective 4 – Evidence-Based Practice	71
8. Four Perspectives Culture	83
9. Barriers to Innovation	92
10. You Can Do This!	97

THERE ARE NOT ENOUGH HOURS IN THE DAY

It was time for the monthly check-in with Anjali to discuss progress with implementation of a grant at her school. Upon arriving, it became clear to me it had been a busy morning for the administrators. Multiple students were sitting outside of Anjali's office, a counselor was on the phone with what sounded like a frustrated parent, and the office secretary was responding to a call from a classroom teacher for an administrator to assist her. Despite these events, Anjali welcomed me and my team from the central office to the conference room. Looking frazzled, she sighed loudly and said, "OK, what are we meeting today for?" We all laughed sympathetically, knowing that this was not the best time for a meeting about the grant. Unfortunately, if we had waited for a good day, we would have been waiting for a long time.

Anjali was a kind person who wanted to do right by her school, students, and parents. She worked long days, even rescheduling personal appointments in order to support the needs of her staff when they asked. Supporting school culture was tremendously important to her and so when teachers complained about not being supported, this surprised and upset her. She was the kind of principal who made time to listen to teachers when they came to her, purchased resources to the best of her ability, and was open to new ideas. With student achievement results being hard-won, teachers felt overworked and underappreciated – as did Anjali.

Anjali's work as an administrator had seen notable changes in recent years. Student needs were different and resulted in calls for help to her and other administrators on a daily basis. Family expectations of the school had also changed. There were more requests for parent-teacher conferences, more advocates attending Individualized Education Plan (IEP) meetings, and more phone calls and emails to Anjali and her teachers. Anjali would at times comment that it was exhausting to be a principal: "Regardless of what I do, I can't seem to move the needle on this problem." Buying resources, giving her teachers as much help as she could, and attending to school culture did not seem to be enough. And the worst part was that she felt like she was frequently chasing her tail to complete tasks on deadline.

Her struggle was palpable. And she's not alone. School principals are increasingly responsible for having the answers to what authors of *Design Your Life,* Bill Burnett and Dave Evans, call "wicked problems." A "wicked problem" is the kind of problem that once solved has a solution that likely can never be useful again, because the problem keeps evolving. And this complexity is only compounded by the staggering 192 tasks that embody the average principal's responsibilities as reported in a 2020 Learning Policy Institute report.

The challenges that Anjali faces daily do not have one simple solution but often result in a singular cry for help from teachers and school staff. Studies claim as many as 50 percent of teachers report that they are not supported by school administration, yet I have not encountered these principals. Many of the principals I know are themselves overworked, doing their best, and regularly asking for help from others.

It is no surprise that the role of education leaders is much different than in prior generations. So too are the differences in our students, families, and communities. We are changing at a rapid pace all while the structures of education stay largely rooted in ways of being from past lifetimes.

As our world changes, education leaders, like yourself, are asked to captain a ship that is trying to make a ninety-degree turn. Uneasy, confusing, and at times violent, this ship demands its captain to maintain a vigilant watch, to guide with minute-by-minute course corrections, and to put all else behind him/her. The world is watching as education leaders navigate great social upheavals. How do we protect students and teachers and our communities as we learn to respect and value those who are different from us? How do we continue to grow to our potential in the midst of an international pandemic? How do we embrace the coming changes while stewarding a crew that is unclear, unprepared, and sometimes unwilling to travel the new course?

One of the greatest challenges of current education leaders is the lack of preparation of teachers and education team members in addressing the complex and individual needs of students. In a report by the Economic Policy Institute published in 2019, the authors report increased numbers of students coming to school unprepared to learn and parents struggling to be meaningfully involved as reasons that the working environment for teachers is so tough. Countless hours of teachers' days are spent managing behavior, reteaching instruction to struggling students, and responding to frantic parents who are rightfully scared for the future well-being of their children. Countless hours of an administrator's time, your time, are also spent managing behavior, responding to parents, and guiding instructional planning for struggling students.

On the day of my meeting with Anjali, one of the students who had been sent to the office had his head down and was kicking the leg of the desk. I commented to Anjali, "Josh just got to the office?" Anjali quickly remarked, "No, he's been here for twenty minutes.

He's finally calmed down!" Before we had arrived, he'd been crying and yelling that his teacher wasn't fair, that he didn't do anything and that she hated him. Josh is a student with a disability in reading, but clearly there's more to his situation than just difficulty in reading. Josh receives a reading intervention daily and has made continuous progress, but as a third-grader, his success in the classroom has required the support of administration far too regularly. Josh's needs go beyond a reading intervention.

The life of an education leader, like Anjali, is that of managing a constant barrage of calls for help with students like Josh, whether real or pseudo emergencies. These calls steal minutes from every hour and impact your ability to lead. Anjali is aware that a significant culprit in this daily assault on her time is the limited knowledge of teachers and education team members on how to help students who learn differently or who have come to school unprepared to learn. Researchers, nonprofit education think-tanks, and policymakers alike recognize this pervasive problem. Why are teachers unprepared to support this kind of learner? Is it that we do not adequately prepare teachers for the job they must do? Is it that we do not pay teachers sufficiently and therefore attract less qualified candidates into the field? Or is it that we do not have the right tools to teach with? The reason may be all of these and more. Education is an increasingly complex system with increasingly complex problems.

Anjali knows that the needs of her students and their families and the expectations of her system and state leaders put heavy value on the role of principal. Principals are supposed to have all of the answers. Anjali openly laments this perspective. "How can I know how to help every student especially in today's environment?" Anjali knows that large social movements occurring across the nation and the world means that the school leader needs more and more skills and knowledge to solve problems effectively. The scope of current changes is daunting. The individual voice is growing louder and demanding that schools see the unique needs and contributions of each student and adjust educational offerings accordingly. This is a tall order for systems that are not ready to pivot to new ways of doing business.

As a school leader you want to be prepared to respond swiftly, yet you have only so many hours in a day and the shifts that are occurring in education demand close attention. You are asked to usher in a culture of acceptance and address the hatred that seems to arise spontaneously when differences of opinion are present; to create an environment that promotes healthy social-emotional development in a world that has reduced the opportunities for children to naturally develop these skills; to be the leader that guides through knowledge, vision, and understanding. Instead, you are the leader who is tied to your office managing student behavior, meeting with teachers to address frustrated parents, and perpetually explaining why things will be better in the future to district leaders and parents alike.

You are vital for the success of your school, but on your own, it's too much to manage. Intuitively you know that your teachers and education team can rise to the challenges of education today. They can solve many student problems without needing your constant direction, all the while finding greater satisfaction in their work. They do not need you to rescue them as often as you currently do.

You know this is true. I know it is, too. Einstein's apt comment that we cannot solve our problems with the same thinking we used when we created them feels like it was created just for this time in history! I invite you to a conversation meant just for you. A conversation that has at its essence a true desire to help education leaders as they prepare their teachers, their teams, and their school community for the challenges of today and tomorrow.

Today's education crisis cannot be solved by buying more programs, by demonizing teachers, education team members, or even parents, by blaming others, or by becoming the problem-solver in chief! Today's education crisis – your education crisis – demands that education evolve to support the most challenging, neglected, and -frustrated students. Today's education crisis needs leaders, like you, who are willing to see the problem through a new set of eyes and, in the process, show those you lead new ways to effectively solve problems.

In embracing the opportunity to partner on an initiative with me, Anjali learned new skills critical to the twenty-first-century educator and leader. She has a structure for addressing student success and challenges that is less personal and relies on proven effective strategies for helping children to learn. Most importantly, she has confidence that her teachers have the foundational knowledge to help today's learners and they have a support system to help them solve problems that stretch their skillset. Anjali's efforts in acquiring these skills are paying off both for herself, with more time to lead, and for her school's diverse student group that her teachers are now empowered to help.

In this book, I'd like to share with you these solutions I've helped so many schools like Anjali's to implement. I know there is a way out of this educational crisis. Will you join me on a journey toward this dream-come-true?

STOP ADMIRING THE PROBLEM

Shortly before my thirty-ninth birthday, I discovered that I had been bitten by a tick. Living in southern Maryland for most of my life, this was not an unusual occurrence. If you like to be outdoors, you are likely to encounter a tick here or there each season. This time *was* different, however. A few days after I had removed the tick the telltale bullseye rash developed around the site of the bite. Feeling fortunate to have noticed the rash, as many never do, I promptly saw my doctor and started a thirty-day regimen of antibiotics. I had done the right thing at the right time and knew that all would be fine. This was not to be the case, however.

By the end of the thirty-day treatment, I had developed vision problems, ringing in my ears, and a sudden numbness over most of my body except for the red-hot pins and needles sensation in my fingers and toes. This launched a series of doctor's appointments with various experts from neurologists to infectious disease specialists and rheumatologists. After nearly three months and crushing diagnoses like rheumatoid arthritis and multiple sclerosis, my doctors finally settled on the seemingly obvious reason for my odd collection of symptoms – Lyme disease. I traveled the common path of oral antibiotics that progressed to IV PICC line antibiotics without relief. My symptoms grew in number and gravity. After nine months of the best care from skilled doctors following the CDC recommendations for effective treatment, I was suffering from significant joint pain, memory loss, and fatigue, and was beginning to have difficulty speaking and swallowing.

Seeking further medical help, I found a doctor who was having success in pushing symptoms into remission with long-term antibiotic use. This doctor discovered that I had two tick-borne parasites in my system, the Lyme bacteria and babesia, and tailored a very particular treatment regimen. With antibiotics, herbal supplements, and slight dietary changes, my symptoms did recede. But a new problem quickly took center stage – whenever I stopped the antibiotics, my symptoms would flood back worse than before. I felt helpless. I was raising two children, teaching at the local college, and working as an inclusion resource teacher in the special education department of the central office for my school system. Life was demanding, yet I knew I could not take antibiotics for the rest of my life. My doctors and others I consulted were resigned to the likelihood that I was going to live the rest of my life with a condition called post-Lyme-disease syndrome. This syndrome looked frustratingly like Lyme disease! I was at the end of my rope, scared about my current situation and for what would lie ahead for my future. On top of that, I felt like a failure.

It's pretty easy to meet people in my area who have been bitten by a tick or who had a brief run-in with Lyme disease symptoms. I heard often how successful their treatments were, that they only took one course of antibiotics and were fine afterward. Questions circled my mind for months. Why was I not experiencing the same success? Why was I failing? Eventually, and more importantly, why did they succeed when I couldn't?!

This new question, "Why did they succeed when I couldn't?" was the impetus for a solution that was there all the time, but I could not see it. For years – three to be exact – I had been admiring the problem. I could tell you everything about my problem – when it started, what it looked like, what to do to avoid it in the future, who were the best doctors, what were the treatments for it … everything. I had been focusing on the problem and then looking to someone else to fix my problem. Doctors needed to find the right medicine, researchers needed to figure out better treatments, and local communities needed to stop deforestation which pushed deer from within woods to the outskirts of communities all the while increasing the likelihood of disease transmission.

This new question was a different question than those I'd been asking previously. This new question acknowledged the problem existed, but it also pointed me in a direction for a solution. Why did they succeed? What did they do that allowed for healing?

The end of my Lyme disease story is that I did recover through changes to my lifestyle in terms of diet, exercise, and stress reduction. It was miraculous. And a solution that was within financial reach to me and my family. It did not require me to be an expert in medicine, health, or nutrition. Instead, the act of trying something that others had tried and doing it on my own created a kind of success that had built within it a generativity of sorts. It unleashed the ultimate growth mindset. One success encouraged another success and another success until I reached a new reality – one that recognized the collaborative nature of health. I am equally, if not more, responsible for my health and healing as is my doctor. This stands in stark contrast to where my journey started – someone else is responsible for healing me.

This lesson about responsibility and change of perspective is as true for you and your teachers as it was for my healing journey. Your teachers and education team members are equally, if not more, responsible for students' achievement and nonacademic success as their principal or education leader. In my story, I made the mistake of thinking that answers lay elsewhere. Teachers make the same mistake over and over. "Principals need to fix this situation."

"Parents need to fix this situation." "I have done all I can do; it's someone else's job to fix this."

I have not met a student, a teacher, or a school that could not improve. We are part of an ever-changing system, for better or worse, and as such, change is simply part of the package. You are leading a diverse group of educators and education staff, some who have embraced change by putting themselves into ever more complex instructional settings and others who have grown capable through deep exploration in a few places and positions over time. I am of the former group.

My graduate training as a speech-language pathologist set me on a course to solve problems for individuals with complex communication needs. Speech-language pathology is a field that was crafted for deep examination to understand the causes and effects of diseases and disabilities on our ability to communicate. Why is this student struggling to produce sounds and words? Why is this student unable to comprehend the teacher's directions and the stories his class is reading? Why does this student use words and gestures so ineffectively when interacting with peers? I found speech-language pathology to be a useful profession to students, parents, and teachers so that we could better understand *why* the student was struggling. *Helping* the student, however, was much more difficult.

In one school, I learned how the curriculum creates a barrier to students resolving speech and language difficulties. To better understand this barrier, I became trained in reading interventions and opened a private practice, discovering that parents felt helpless and lacked the ability to effectively collaborate with schools. To better understand how to help increase parent involvement, I became an IEP Facilitator and, in the process, learned that teachers, both general and special education, struggled to navigate the demands of teaching a grade-level curriculum and understand the individual needs of each student within their classrooms. This led me to the central office of my school system where I have served in many roles, written and implemented grants large and small, and led teams at the state, local, and school levels all with the same aim – to help struggling students and struggling educators find success.

Along the way, I honed my own communication skills through teaching both at the undergraduate and graduate levels and accepting every opportunity to speak nationally, at the state level, and within my own district – with one clear message threaded through each presentation: With a slight shift in thinking and a few tools in their toolbox, teachers and other education team members can take equal responsibility for their students' achievement and nonacademic success in school as their principal or another education leader or a parent. You are the answer you are looking for. The magic bullet you are looking for is you. Well, perhaps that's not the right metaphor given the speed with which a magic bullet "solves problems."

IT TAKES TIME AND COLLABORATION

History has shown us how significant problems can be resolved by allowing enough time to thoroughly understand the problem before acting on a solution. Author Ryan Holiday, in *Stillness Is the Key*, wrote about the Cuban Missile Crisis in 1962. President Kennedy refused to act quickly, rejecting the pressure from defense leaders. Instead, he insisted that his team take time to think about this situation from every perspective. The Cuban Missile Crisis was resolved not through force, but through understanding the perspective of the Russian leaders toward the world. Education is not such a high-stakes game, but it is one that involves pressure to fix problems quickly whether or not that is the right approach.

As grant leader, I was invited, with my team, to attend the state Department of Education's conference featuring a national expert in mathematics. My school district had been implementing a State Personnel Development Grant (SPDG) that focused on narrowing the achievement gap in elementary mathematics between students without disabilities and students with disabilities. The session was organized with some lectures and lots of hands-on interactive activities and discussions. Participants were encouraged to share their answers and to comment on this experience solving problems through this new lens. As with most professional development activities, some participants engaged fully in the activities and others minimally engaged. My team, which included four instructional coaches, two general education teachers, two special education teachers, and myself, dove into the math activities. It was fun and interesting to learn new ways to understand how and why students do what they do in solving problems. The group of us engaged in lots of animated conversation. Leading the way, I volunteered our group to share our findings and discussion as often as we could. I called for the presenter to join our group, help us see what we couldn't see. It was my job, as the group's leader, to be certain each of our members got the maximum benefit from this opportunity. By the end of the day, our group had developed a reputation as "rock stars," a reputation that would precede us for years to come, much to the chagrin of other districts, I'm sure. Our group had developed, through our grant activities, operating standards that we all agreed to engage with. Today's meeting called for "Engage with Enthusiasm" and as the team leader, I did just that. At the end of the day, feeling successful in bringing value to my team, we headed to our hotel rooms with a plan to meet up later that evening.

A few hours later, I joined my co-liaison and the grant's math coach in the lobby. They were talking intensely and seemed bothered. I asked, "What's up?" Chris responded, "We are hearing that there's confusion and frustration about today's workshop. The teachers are worried that they will be asked to implement this new method. How are they supposed to do this? What was the State thinking when they asked us to attend? We already have a new program we are implementing!" The level of concern was evident. As a team, we worked hard to be responsive to our colleagues who were implementing the work. Effective implementation in multiple schools across multiple grade levels is not just hard work, it is, as our state lead Marilyn would sometimes say, "messy work." Messy, yes, impossible, no. Oftentimes when the stress levels of staff rise, a sort of admiration for the problem develops. We are so good at finding facts and evidence to support our problem, with fact after fact strengthening the rightness of the claim that we can't see any way out of the problem. It's a vicious cycle and rarely leaves those involved feeling optimistic. It seemed that we were at risk of getting stuck in this type of admiration.

Given the scope of our effort through SPDG, it was important for the grant leaders to be trained to support the work at the classroom, school, and district levels. I, along with a few others, was trained in systems coaching by Barbara Sims with UNC Chapel Hill. Systems coaching takes a systems lens to understanding, predicting, resolving, and avoiding problems. In the current situation, I wanted our teachers to realize the benefit of having attended the training. It was high-quality professional development with evidence-based methods that would help teachers -provide individualized instruction for students, particularly those with disabilities. It could be infused within the current model, but if I simply told them things were fine, the teachers may have felt unheard and even attacked.

Using implementation science frameworks, I recommended we add the teachers' concerns to the agenda for the upcoming school-based implementation team meetings – an action that would be a type of facilitative administration. At the meeting, I provided an overview of the concern and worked with the team to proactively look for ways to effectively address the challenges that the teachers had presented. We agreed that certain teachers who had expressed interest would be supported by the math coaches to explore these new strategies. The outcomes of the trials could be shared within and between schools.

Following the implementation team meeting, one teacher did try the new mathematics strategy and asked for me to talk with her about the outcomes. We discovered that most of her students had a readiness for the next lesson, but a few students demonstrated that they would need concrete representation supports. It was an aha moment for this teacher that allowed the coming week's lesson plans to be slightly adjusted to give better access to the content for the two students. While not perfect, it was a start and now this teacher had a better understanding of how she could develop more inclusive lesson plans. Powerful.

On the surface, this may not sound like much. It is without question though, significant. Teachers are asked to implement new practices frequently – from new curriculums to new behavior systems. They are always in a state of learning. When teachers express frustration with the workload of education, they are likely feeling the weight of learning new skills on top of managing the day-to-day work of teaching. It is with these small insights, however, that changes in how we teach move closer to the ideal where students of varying skill levels and needs can find success within the classroom. As an education leader, you are always balancing the needs of the school against the concerns and complaints of teachers and parents. In the changing world of education, leaders will be using dialogue and conversation skills differently to help teachers and teams move beyond admiring the problem so that incrementally we grow effective teacher competencies. And this takes and deserves time.

In my first year as a resource teacher, I followed an experienced instructional specialist as the special education resource for a high school that had been trying to bring about effective co-teaching for a number of years. "I provided my teachers expensive, high-quality professional development. Why aren't they using it?" the administrator assigned to special education of a local high school said to me. The teacher teams, a general education teacher and a special education teacher, had been offered paid after-school training for at least two years. The teachers knew what co-teaching was and the basics of how to do it, but impromptu check-ins by the administrator found that only one co-teaching pair regularly engaged in high-impact co-teaching practices. The other classrooms utilized the less effective co-teaching model of one teach-one assist. It felt on the surface like the teachers were deliberately choosing not to use the more effective models. Teachers, however, felt that the co-teaching expectations did not take into account the significant needs of the students and that the special education teacher needed to be free to individualize everything for select students. It was an "us versus them" situation.

I worked with the administrator to develop a plan that could be presented to the principal and prepared for roll-out in September of the coming school year. Recognizing that the teachers were not directly opposing this work, but rather needed more support to step into it, we developed the plan through the lens of implementation science. We proposed setting up a co-teaching implementation team that would track data regarding implementation and student achievement as well as be the cheerleaders for the work, focusing on training that included feedback to the teachers on their application of the skills and opportunities to observe effective co-teaching at their school and at other schools. It was a comprehensive plan that recognized the problem was not simply that teachers were not implementing the co-teaching methods. It was a plan that recognized the underlying systems that were influencing the reason why the work did not previously take off.

So often we underestimate the benefit that we'll gain by engaging collaboratively. Ulrich Boser writes in *Learn Better* that, "... diverse groups promote richer forms of thinking. When we're with people who are different than us, we are more likely to engage in complex thought." And just as important are the skills of engaging through systems thinking perspective. When we have a clear understanding of the barriers to success, we are better positioned to act and succeed. Systems thinking and implementation science provide structure and permission for administrators to think and act differently to solve problems.

Large-scale change, like the change that may be needed in your school, takes planning and preparation. Most of us dive into this aspect of change work with verve. The launch of projects feels invigorating until the first hiccup surfaces. Problems with implementation always arise. Consider a simple book study for your staff. You've selected a current topic that is relevant to the needs of your school. The first thing you become aware of is that some of the staff think it's a waste of time. You've given up your staff meetings in order to provide time for your school to come together around this important topic, but inevitably, a group of teachers can't make it to some of the meetings or emergency parent-teacher conferences take priority. As you carry on with the book study, you notice that some groups are actively engaged in the discussion. They've come prepared. Others are not participating. Problems with implementation always arise! Large-scale change takes time and so investment and planning across school years are needed if you are to realize the true benefit of the professional development or book study you have brought to your staff.

Some of the teachers from the math professional development experience I mentioned earlier are from a local Title I school. I had the great privilege to work with teachers and administrators at this school as we looked to narrow achievement gaps. This team worked hard to bring into being new educational models. Holding a clear vision for this school, I regularly worked with the math coaches to resolve barriers to implementation of the evidence-based practices. Having invested four years in intense learning, a new principal was assigned to the school. She came with energy, new ideas, and clear expectations that she layered onto the existing practices. A few years later, this school was recognized as a National ESEA Distinguished School. Preparing teachers to take learning and success to the next level is sophisticated work that requires time for teachers to learn the new practices and recognize them as those that their students need most.

After years of supporting state and local initiatives, writing and leading grants, and helping teachers and related service providers resolve disputes with parents and improve student performance, I began to notice recurring trends in the interactions I was having across all levels. Teachers and other education staff do not have a broad enough or deep enough skillset to independently address the extent of needs in their classrooms. National, state, and local leadership, in an attempt to help, recommend programs, but these programs tend to be implemented through a one-size-fits-all approach. With national movements such as Black Lives Matter, disability rights efforts, and calls for equity and equality for marginalized groups, education is oftentimes at the center of reform discussions. Even when our programs instruct us to form small groups that are in theory more individualized, there are inherent flaws in the rationale that would have us believe all of the students within that small group have the same need. I find myself repeating the same information often. The context that the student lives within is important. What are the systems that are impacted by the student's struggle? What individual strengths and weaknesses contribute to their experience? Who are you working with to find solutions? Are you communicating through a lens of inclusivity, possibility, and understanding?

In deciding to write this book, my hope is that I can shed light on areas that when understood and applied immeasurably benefit both the teacher and the student. I am witness to the sadness and anxiety of our education team members, and I believe lack of knowledge in key areas is part of the reason. These unprecedented times demand that educators develop an understanding of the framework of education. The basics needed to be effective as an educator have grown. Teachers are struggling as much as their students. As an administrator, you may know the importance of teamwork, systems thinking, individualizing instruction for the diverse classroom, and evidence-based practices that catapult learning, but I can tell you, many, if not all of your teachers and education staff do not understand nor apply this knowledge to help solve problems, reduce stress, and establish effective learning communities within your school. This is not a condemnation of teachers and education professionals. Rather, it is a recognition that education has changed at a rapid pace. How could teachers have been prepared for times like these? Many of us personally have not been ready to face the challenges of these times! I want this book to be a resource for you as you build the twenty-first century school beyond this point. I know you see a future where your school operates more systematically and inclusively so that all learners, including those from diverse backgrounds and who have disabilities, can experience success. I do too. I've glimpsed it in working with so many amazing teachers, speech-language pathologists, principals, coaches, directors, and state leaders. Solving the challenges that keep you tied to your desk or running to rescue a teacher does not help you to move our schools into the next phase. I offer this book as a contribution to the work that lies ahead for you, as a guide to the places where you can look for answers.

    In my career, I have learned three tremendously important lessons. All students can learn. All education staff can gain new professional skills. All schools can make radical changes. These three are absolutely true when education leaders, from principals and vice-principals to instructional coaches and district leaders, recognize the problem without getting stuck in defining it as good or bad and allow space (time) for a possible solution to emerge. One of the greatest joys in my professional life has been helping teams to overcome adversity to help students and allow solutions to emerge. The magic of the classroom is a marvel to watch in action!

LET'S GET YOU BACK TO YOUR WORK

Seeing a problem through a new lens is tricky. Our perspectives are based on our knowledge and experiences. This is true in our personal lives as well as our professional lives. Gaining a new perspective on a topic or problem starts with an awareness that others see our situation differently. Some people pick ideas up through experiences with others. In the professional world where there are many voices competing for teachers' attention, it can be difficult to recognize new ideas or solutions without opportunities for dedicated training, application, and reflection.

Throughout my career, I've been accused of being "too optimistic." This always makes me laugh because I am not optimistic, but I have experienced lots of success of all kinds in my life. Not easy success, but the kind of success you experience from perseverance. I know that if I keep trying, I'll learn more and understand better so that the odds of the outcome being positive is quite good. At this point in my career, I know that when barriers present themselves, they are not the end of the story. My perspectives around helping, solving problems, and innovating are enriched by the conversations I have every day with school leaders like you.

The pedagogical basis of education is deep, and with the inability of universities to sufficiently support teachers in the development of foundational skills, expanding the perspective of teachers falls on principals and school systems. As you read, you will learn about the Four Perspectives that empower teachers and education team members to help struggling learners of all kinds.

In Chapter 4, I introduce Perspective 1: Effective Teams. As teachers leave the workforce in alarming numbers, a top reason is a perceived lack of support. The burden of meeting the ever-expanding responsibility in the classroom, both in person and virtually, demands a diverse lens through which to understand the struggling learner. As school leaders embrace teams and collaboration, the effectiveness of these collaborations is called into question. The research on collaboration challenges our understanding of the readiness of teachers and education team members to successfully solve problems together. Teams who have developed skills such as interprofessional communication and use of data for reflection are better equipped for dynamic and collaborative practice. As Steve Jobs once remarked that things in business are never done by one person. I think this is true in education, too.

In Chapter 5, I present Perspective 2: Systems Thinking. As teachers seek to resolve issues with students and families, critical mistakes are often made due to a lack of understanding of the various systems the student, the teacher, and the family are operating within. When teachers are told that they must accommodate a challenging student in the classroom, it is hard for many to understand why. Teachers and teams who utilize systems thinking address barriers through a process lens. Dr. Shikumar Rao, former business school professor, teaches leaders that we should look at life as a civil engineer does. Challenges in the environment are not bad, they are just a "part of a construction site." Systems thinking will help teachers develop a deeper understanding of the educational landscape they are navigating.

In Chapter 6, I outline Perspective 3: The Diverse Classroom. All skilled educators know that the first step in solving problems is understanding the problem. Just as our students can select irrelevant information or misunderstand signals that point us in the direction of what the problem is actually asking, so too do educators and parents rely on limited and sometimes unreliable data to make decisions upon. The famous American psychologist Abraham Maslow stated, "If the only tool you have is a hammer, you tend to see every problem as a nail." When teachers are provided a deeper understanding of the variability in the domains of development in the student within their classrooms, teachers are more equipped to select the right solution to the problems their students are experiencing.

In Chapter 7, I uncover Perspective 4: Evidence-Based Practice, my favorite topic! Not all instructional practices are equal. Education leaders are aware of the constant drum beat from state and national leaders regarding the use of evidence-based practices (EBPs). Wading through the barrage of programs, curriculums, and processes to select only the best EBPs for your students, it is hard to understand why, with all of these resources, student performance has not significantly improved. Although programs do help point teachers in the right direction, the actual magic of the classroom exists in the teacher pedagogy. The interactions between teachers, students, and the learning environment and learning tasks are improved or diminished by the set of EBPs a teacher has within his/her teacher tool bag. Teachers who know which practices are more likely to improve student performance show greater improvement than those who do not.

In Chapter 8, I discuss how to bring these perspectives to your staff through training, implementation, and monitoring. I offer suggestions for how to structure your plan and provide an alternative model that spreads training out over the course of a year. In Chapter

9, I review barriers that you will likely encounter as you begin this critical work.

These Four Perspectives reflect the knowledge that successful teachers and teams understand. It is through these perspectives that I have helped students, teachers, and teams and led colleagues. Richard Haight in *The Warrior's Meditation* wrote, "My martial arts teacher in Japan – Shizen Osaki, a master instructor of multiple samurai arts – often says that the secret to mastery is found in the basics ... and becoming a teacher myself, I too have noticed people's tendency to skim over the basics and in doing so, miss vital elements that cause them to struggle more than they would otherwise." In today's schools, these Four Perspectives are the basics that all educators must know. Teaching the curriculum is not enough. Our diverse classrooms and changing communities will rely on the teacher to solve dynamic problems, ones that are not resolved by a trip to the principal's office.

As schools embrace the awareness of the need for more preparation for teachers to effectively manage a classroom, implement a curriculum, and support the growth and well-being of a diverse student body, new knowledge gaps in our teachers' readiness are being revealed. This book is a guide for the education leader to begin to fill these gaps in ways that will increase the capacity of teachers to effectively problem solve without you.

PERSPECTIVE 1 – EFFECTIVE TEAMS

After years of working in the public schools in many different roles, you are likely to have experienced at one time or another an opportunity to work with a high-performing team. You can find these throughout education from overachieving grade-level teams to effective interdisciplinary IEP teams to Relay for Life committees. When teams come together in just the right way, the outcomes achieved by a few people can seem impossible/fantastical and honestly, may even be frustrating to those on the outside of these teams. In one school I worked with, I remember every person who was on our grant committee from that school said at one point or another, "That fifth-grade team doesn't need any help. They are amazing!" It is obvious that high-performing teams function differently than other teams. What's less obvious is how these teams come to be high-performing.

The message of teams and collaboration is nothing new. You are encouraged to implement team structures such as Professional Learning Communities (PLCs) and implementation teams as part of programs like PBIS (Positive Behavior Interventions and Supports), and under every rock you turn over for how to help teachers improve achievement for students you will find collaborative activities of one sort or another are recommended. We get it. Collaboration is important!

Yet, if collaboration is as powerful as it is toted to be, why are we struggling with the same challenges year after year? Surely decades of collaboration should align with national improvements in student reading scores or improve teacher retention. Instead, we see near stagnant NAEP (National Assessment of Educational Progress) scores with 35 percent of fourth-grade students reading at or above proficient levels. Teacher turnover rates were reported to be 16 percent of teachers annually by the National Center for Education Statistics. These statistics are horrifying! I'm sure you are wondering: where's the bang for the buck?

I am here to tell you that despite the lackluster numbers, effective collaboration is at the heart of every success story I have ever experienced and if you look closely, you will find the same is true in your school and in your personal experiences. Learning to collaborate involves the development of a set of skills. In 2017, Gallup found, for example, that skills necessary for effective collaboration include "communicating, engaging in conflict resolution so that projects stay on target, listening to fellow team members, and persuading team members." And individuals will possess varying degrees of competency with these skills, just like we see with development of a teaching repertoire.

Effective collaboration goes beyond the development of soft skills. These ideas, while relatively new to education, are much more highly developed in other sectors including the technology community. The concept of agile teams, a scaled-up version of an implementation team, has as a core belief a recognition in the value of collaboration of members across disciplines to solve problems. Essentially, small multidisciplinary agile teams come together to solve an identified problem quickly. The members of the team identify who and what resources are needed to solve problems, often breaking the problem into small steps. The team then mobilizes to put solutions into place. As described in a 2018 *Harvard Business Review*, when "confronted with a large, complex problem, they break it into modules, develop solutions to each component through rapid prototyping and tight feedback loops, and integrate the solutions into a coherent whole." Basically, agile teams use protocols for team performance. Each member of the team develops and operates through a set of core competencies.

I have found that effective collaboration is not optional if you want to create an environment that can overcome big challenges. And effective collaboration can and should be nurtured. In my experience, helping teachers to develop core competencies for effective interdisciplinary collaboration is one of the easier areas that can be improved. Rarely are the core competencies new with most teachers having a basic understanding. Each core competency, however, can be endlessly developed. As a leader, you too have had to develop deeper levels of knowledge!

Below I outline an introductory framework for *core competencies* that can help teams move from poor or mediocre to high achieving. Let's dive into these four core competencies your teams should develop and employ.

CORE COMPETENCIES FOR EFFECTIVE TEAMS

Research tells us that effective teams come together around shared values and ethics, common definitions of roles and responsibilities, interprofessional communication expectations, teamwork, and learning and critical reflection. In my work with teacher teams, our shared values and ethics to seek solutions rather than "admire the problem" (as Michelle Harris of the Instructional Coaching Group teaches) helped us to stay efficient with our time and remain student-centered. We asked questions about who could help with each need identified and so dispersed the work throughout the group. We identified logistics around team communication and reflection. We took a team approach.

TEAM VALUES AND ETHICS

I received a call from Christine, a speech-language pathologist (SLP). She was a first-year SLP with lots of energy and excitement to be in her first job. Today, however, Christine was crying. A few weeks earlier, I had met with a few SLPs to ask if they would be willing to bring a Response to Intervention (RTI) model for speech and language concerns to their schools. Christine agreed. Following this meeting, a teacher stopped her in the hall to ask her to screen a kindergarten student in her classroom. She said, "He's having trouble producing sounds and he's hard to understand." Christine responded with, "This is perfect! Let's talk. I'll come down after school and show you a few things." That afternoon, Christine met with three kindergarten teachers and explained the RTI model and provided examples of what she'd like the teachers to do to help the students with speech concerns. The teachers were furious and lashed out at Christine. This was a valuable lesson to me. In RTI, the teacher and the SLP become a team, working together to address the needs of the student in the least intrusive manner possible. I had not provided Christine or the teachers she was supporting with the tools to work together effectively.

Effective teams will come together around common values and ethics. But these values and ethics cannot be uncovered unless we purposely seek to discover them. Just as teachers unpack with students the meaning of abstract words like "respect," so do teacher teams need to unpack attitudes and beliefs about the work they are to engage in together. Christine had no way of knowing that the teachers would become so upset about RTI for speech and language. And once in this difficult situation, she did not have the tools to resolve the conflict that had arisen.

UNPACKING TEAM VALUES AND ETHICS

Provide teams with the following questions/prompts to discuss. These are considered both personally and from the context of the team's purpose. You can use formal means to explore topics including accountability, respect, confidentiality, trust, integrity, honest, ethical behavior, equity, commitment, and engagement by using questions like these.

1. What is the purpose of your team? Why is it important for this team to come together for this stated purpose?

2. What does respect look like? Provide three or four examples.

3. How does appreciation for cultural diversity and individual differences feel?

4. Discuss the role of honesty and openness with team members.

5. Is it important to be able to count on one another? Why or why not?

What I do is when I put teams together, I don't just tell them they are going to work together. I tell them they are going to create magic together. I tell them that we are going to learn about ourselves and learn about each other and we are going to love this time together. And we make sure to laugh and smile through the whole thing. We are uncovering our values and ethics.

I want teams to get to know each other and to commit to a goal together. I want them to learn to be vulnerable with each other and for the team to come to a place where they learn to care for each other's sensibilities. Team members need to see each other as people.

- What's important to you?

- What hobbies do you engage in?

- What TV shows/movies do you enjoy?

- Tell me about your family.

- How do you handle stress?

- Why did you become a teacher, speech-language pathologist, counselor, etc.?

- What do you hope to achieve in your career?

- Where do you like to vacation?

- Have you ever been part of an effective team? What made that team effective?

- What do you hope this team can accomplish?

• Does anything make you nervous about the team's purpose?

• How can a team of diverse cultures and experiences work together while embracing differences?

What did you discover about each other? Summarize the big picture. Compare and contrast.

There are no right or wrong answers. Learning about each other creates an environment of connection. "Interprofessional teams that respect the need for 'psychological safety' create an environment in which frank conversations allow discussion of problems, inconsistencies, and even errors without fear of reprisal" according to Blaiser and Nevins, in a writing on interprofessional collaboration. When challenges occur within the group, members of the team have connections that go beyond the current situation. I provided Christine with a simple Venn diagram and three questions as an icebreaker and encouraged her to begin forming a team with her kindergarten teachers. Once she was prepared with tools to develop a shared set of values and ethics, she and the kindergarten teachers grew together and explored the RTI model effectively. By mid-year, Christine was regularly modeling lessons inside the kindergarten classrooms providing the bridge the teachers needed to be able to support speech and language in Tier 1 more successfully on their own.

INTERPROFESSIONAL COMMUNICATION

Saundra and Tasha had been assigned as co-teachers of a fifth-grade reading class. Like many co-teachers, they found out just before school started that they would be in this teaching arrangement. Saundra had previously co-taught with other teachers and was not thrilled to be in this situation again. By the end of September, both teachers were frustrated. The principal asked me to help these two teachers improve in co-teaching. Upon meeting them, it was clear that communication had broken down and neither was listening to the other. During an observation of a lesson, Saundra, the general education teacher, essentially taught the entire lesson. Tasha, the special education teacher, walked around the room, periodically checking in with students. When I asked Tasha why she was not more involved, she went into a fifteen-minute rant about how Saundra didn't respect Tasha, how she would cut Tasha off if she tried to add on in the lesson, and Saundra was treating her like an instructional assistant. From Saundra's perspective, Tasha was so inconsistent in the classroom, being pulled for IEP meetings and to address student behavior in other classrooms, that she could not be trusted to help with teaching.

Interprofessional communication happens when professionals communicate with each other, with students and their families, and with the broader community in a transparent, collaborative, and responsible way. This type of communication promotes trusting, respectful relationships. Mutual respect is essential for interprofessional communication. Respect helps foster a positive environment in which to set shared goals, create collaborative plans, make decisions, and share responsibilities. Saundra and Tasha were not in a respectful, trusting relationship.

Unpacking Interprofessional Communication

Many people take for granted the skills needed for effective communication. Because we talk all the time, we are overconfident that we effectively use this skill and few of us reflect on our own roles in communication breakdowns, and instead focus on the lack of competency in our communication partner. Two basic communication skills that benefit collaboration are active listening and open-ended questioning.

When I work with teachers, related service providers, and other education team members, I want them to know that becoming a skilled communicator takes practice and self-reflection. Providing teachers an opportunity to practice these skills in low-stakes environments, like at a staff meeting or a planned professional development, helps the teachers learn what it sounds like and what it feels like to engage in these practices and ultimately helps with self-reflection.

1. Listening

   a. Active, responsive listening – in pairs, one participant talks for two minutes, the other listens only. The listener signals they are listening with head nods. After two minutes, the participants switch roles. Then, they discuss the following questions.

   i. How did it feel to simply listen to each other?
   ii. Did you find yourself slipping into autobiographical listening, where a memory was triggered and you were not attending to the speaker?
   iii. Did you find it hard not to respond to the speaker's words immediately?

   b. Summarizing the speaker's words – in pairs, one participant talks for two minutes, the other listens only. When the time is up, the listener repeats back or summarizes what he/she thinks was understood. After two minutes, they switch roles and try again. Then, they discuss the following questions.

i. How did it feel to listen and summarize?
ii. How was this different than simply active listening?
iii. How would this benefit you to include this skill in your team meetings?

2. Questioning

a. Open-ended questions – in pairs, teachers formulate open-ended questions to better understand the role or perspective of their partner on the team. For example, Saundra might ask Tasha, "What can we do to keep you in class more consistently?" In a staff meeting or in a professional development setting, you could choose to develop this skill by addressing values and ethics. After teachers have practiced asking questions to discover more about their partner, it is critical that they reflect with questions like these.

i. What did it look like, sound like, feel like to use or be asked an open-ended question?
ii. How can this help me in my collaboration discussions?

Although we use listening and questioning in everyday communication, most of the time, we are distracted listeners, listening to respond to the other and seeking out moments for our perspectives and values to be heard. We shut down what the other is trying to communicate. By giving the speaker more space to share their knowledge and thoughts on a situation, we can uncover solutions that previously lay buried. I helped Saundra and Tasha overcome this frustrating situation with strategies for team building, including interprofessional communication skills. While it is possible to repair damaged relationships, it is a much better idea to nurture them from the start with continued practice in core competencies such as interprofessional communication.

TEAM EXPECTATIONS AND GOALS

In a collaboration between pre-K general education, pre-K special education, and speech-language pathology, I brought teachers together in regional teams to facilitate the emergence of Phonological Processing instruction in the classroom. There was limited time for these teams to meet. Pulling teachers from the classroom is never easy and having them drive to neighboring schools was doubly problematic. It was important that these meetings were focused on the goals, whether or not I, or someone from the central office, could be there.

At the launch of this grant, I put teachers, SLPs, and instructional assistants into their regional teams, provided them examples from the Boundless Learning Program, and helped them to develop a set of expectations specific to their teams. Then, at each regional meeting, the team started with a review of these expectations and a discussion regarding how the team thought they were doing with each. One team member reached out to me after her second regional meeting. Katie said, "Our team wanted you to know that this is the first time we felt like meetings were really focused and time was not wasted on complaining about things in the classroom. It was weird at first, but talking about our team's expectations before we start every meeting reminds us of these really important things." I was not surprised to hear this. Without agreed-upon operating standards, so much time is wasted in meetings. And while we think complaining or talking about other things will make us feel better, the funny thing is, nothing feels better than successfully accomplishing a goal. Without expectations, we sabotage our potential.

Unpacking Team Expectations and Goals

Effective teams are explicit about the ways they will work together. They identify specific behaviors that members will adhere to. You don't need a lot of expectations, but you need enough to ensure that members understand there is shared responsibility for success of the team. Each member's interactions or lack of interactions impacts the whole group.

1. Uncover personal expectations. In a group, discuss teams that you have been a member of previously.

   a. Think about teams that were effective. What did you notice about how members of these teams interacted, engaged in the work, and demonstrated responsibility for outcomes?
   b. Think about teams that were ineffective. What did you notice about how members of these teams interacted, engaged in the work, and demonstrated responsibility for outcomes?

2. Identify shared expectations.

   a. Individually, write down three qualities of effective teams that are important to you.
   b. As a group, share the qualities you identified and notice any similarities between the two.

c. State three to five expectations that are agreed upon within the group.

3. Write out expectation statements.

a. Turn the three to five expectations into brief expectation statements. For example, if the team said "timeliness" is important, an expectation might be, "As a team, we will arrive and adjourn meetings on time."

4. Set a goal for use of expectations.

a. Select one expectation and write a short-term goal for the team to achieve within the next month or quarter. For example, "We will arrive and adjourn meetings on time for 100 percent of our meetings in September." This step is important. Be sure to make a plan to use these expectations, otherwise, team meetings can become a sort of "checking the box" task.

I want you to know that when teams take the time to uncover, set, and use expectations, teams find greater success. All teams, no matter how small, should engage in this step. By doing this, we are giving each other permission to hold each other accountable to each other and to the team's goals. Katie and her pre-K team members were able to support each other in learning about the new curriculum rather than finding themselves reinforcing ineffective patterns of collaboration. They had expectations such as "listen first," "participate actively," and "complete tasks within the time allotted." Reviewing these before each meeting was a practice that only took moments to engage in, but served as a tool to focus them and gave each other permission to remind others to stay on task.

USING DATA CYCLES

You and your teachers are inundated with the messages of the importance of data. However, your teachers' efforts with data usage may not be as fruitful as researchers suggest it can be.

    We met as a school-based team to establish our team's performance goals. We determined that we wanted to see a ten-point narrowing in the gap between general education and special education students on the end-of-year assessment for a third-grade classroom. In discussing this goal, I asked the team to identify data sources that could help us know if our actions were on the right track toward achieving this goal by the end of the year. It was clear there were no systemic or regularly administered classroom assessments that could be useful. In previous initiatives, I'd experienced moments like this. The team says, "We don't have anything like that," and the conversation stops. Then we wait until the end of the year and see how we did. I knew that we would not meet our target if we were not checking on our progress. It was imperative that we figure this out. The team decided to explore options and bring ideas back to the team at our next meeting. With the help of our grant's math coach, the team put into place a formative assessment structure that was simple to use and hugely informative regarding student progress toward the goal. I knew this team could solve this challenge and they did. At each subsequent meeting, we used a data-informed cycle to look at student achievement and plan for next steps and ask, "are our efforts making a difference?"

    I explain to teams that if we don't look at our performance regularly, we can't realize our potential. Our efforts will essentially be wasted. Establishing routines to look systematically at data to see if our efforts are paying off does not take much time. And the time it does take pays off royally.

UNPACKING USING DATA CYCLES

At its foundation, according to the National Center for Education Statistics, a data cycle is a "recurring timeline for the production, application and reporting of data." Teams use this cycle as a procedure to guide and simplify their interactions with data. Many programs you are likely using recommend engagement in data-informed cycles. Johns Hopkins University Center for Technology in Education teaches a model through their Dynamic Impact Program. The Ongoing Assessment Project (OGAP) teaches a model called the OGAP Professional Learning Community (PLC) model. The Wilson Reading Program embeds formative assessment and summative assessment data review as required components for lesson planning. My point being: this concept is not new.

In my years of supporting teachers and teams, however, it has been one of the hardest aspects of solving problems. During the meeting, it feels like it is taking forever. Who has time to look at the data, write a goal, write action steps, decide who will do what, and assign timelines? It just feels like a lot of unnecessary effort. And at first, it is a lot. Once you have established effective patterns for data analysis, the cycle drives the discussion, and the team is focused on what matters.

Using resources from the Active Implementation Hub developed by the National Implementation Research Network, I recommend you follow the below outlined path.

1. Establish the rationale for data cycles.

a. I share an anecdote from personal experience about the process my car mechanic goes through when he's trying to figure out what the mystery noise is that developed in the rear right quarter panel. He engages in a process of gathering data, filtering the data to the relevant concern, selecting a fix, making a plan to try the fix, trying it, determining if it worked, and if it didn't, he starts the cycle all over again.
b. I then provide research that explains why data cycles help improve performance and I connect this to successful teams I've helped.

i. The reason for much of systems change work is not thoroughly developed and shared with those who will implement the change. When we are unclear about why an innovation is necessary, we tend to climb the "Ladder of Inference" in which our thinking process develops an idea without us consciously realizing it. We want to be sure that teams have enough information about how this process is beneficial to them so that the inference does not become, "It's just one more thing."

2. Present a framework of the data cycle you'd like your team to use.

a. AI Hub Improvement Cycles

i. Plan – identify barriers or challenges and specify how to move forward.
ii. Do – implement the plan as intended.
iii. Study – monitor the process.
iv. Act – use the knowledge gained to improve the process.

3. Allow teams time to consider areas of focus.

    a. During a staff meeting or professional development, group participants in teams that are meaningful to the participants.
    b. Provide time for the team members to determine areas of concern that are interrelated for the team members.

4. Facilitate data analysis and identification of trends in the data.

    a. Provide time for the team to gather data. I recommend you provide the classroom and school-level data so that time of the team members is focused on gathering additional data that is more specific to their particular area of concern.

5. Set a goal to address the data.

    a. Each team should write one or two goals to address the area of concern.

    i. By December, the percentage of students with disabilities who score proficient on the classroom-based assessment will increase by 10 percent.

6. Select the evidence-based practice your team will utilize to address the concern.

    a. In this stage, teams will determine the means through which the goal will be addressed. How will more students improve their proficiency in the area of concern? Teams will benefit from Perspective 4 for this stage found in Chapter 7.

7. Identify action steps to implement the evidence-based practice.

a. Once an evidence-based practice has been selected, teams should write out action steps that include the following:

i. The exact steps
ii. Who will complete this
iii. Timeline for completion
iv. Method of monitoring associated with this step

8. Set a date for the next data cycle. I recommend meeting at least monthly.

As you can tell, learning to engage in data-informed cycles is an activity that will require planning and time. Many schools do not have the ability to complete all eight steps in a single day. If you set a goal to have the eight steps completed within a month and facilitate team meetings for ninety minutes at a time, you will find that this process can be launched sooner than it probably feels right now. Do not be overwhelmed. I assure you that you can do this, and your teachers can too. Putting this structure in place will have tremendous value for you particularly when teams are able to function with more ease and focus. Additionally, it keeps everyone accountable to progress.

The time spent on employing strategies for team building is well worth it. While many argue that there's simply not enough time and teams need to simply complete the task given to them, the reality is that if we put this twenty-first-century skill base aside, the teachers' cries over lack of support will grow louder. Our student bodies are changing at a furious pace and teachers need the voices of others to help see possible solutions, to receive support in learning new practices, to find the profession of education as a hospitable environment to work, and ultimately to learn to effectively manage challenges that arise for their classrooms and individual students.

I will be honest with you. As I said earlier, this is the hardest skill for teachers to learn and use effectively. I have worked with some principals who are masters at this type of thinking and problem-solving. Many, however, do not effectively move beyond Step 5. These first few steps are important, yes, but the power of this process to change student behavior and achievement is in Steps 4 – 8. I have long held that many teachers and education team members know what to do, but without the accountability and support of a well-structured team, good intentions oftentimes go unfulfilled.

You may need to hire a coach to help develop your teams. You may need to designate one of your administrative or instructional coaches as the expert in team-building. You may need to prioritize learning these skills and applying them ruthlessly. What I mean is that when we ask people to do new things, they need reasons why on a regular basis. They need a leader who is unwavering in his/her belief that the team can achieve this outcome. I have helped teams make notable steps forward and I know that without my expertise the status quo would have returned very quickly. Schools are busy, dynamic places with many distractions. I encourage you to unleash the power of collaboration, set a goal to create effective team structures within your school, and give your teachers and education teams the tools they need to resolve problems effectively.

PERSPECTIVE 2 – SYSTEMS THINKING

Historically, education has been structured in silos that compartmentalize students, teachers, and resources. As research began showing the benefits of collaboration for students and teachers, classrooms and teacher planning both saw notable changes. Rows of desks were replaced by desks grouped together in a unit. Individual planning time was enhanced with weekly (or more frequent) grade-level team meetings. Research shows that teamwork is positively related to performance, and so collaboration and teaming are recognized to be more necessary than ever before.

If twenty-first-century educators need more collaboration to increase effectiveness, who are they to collaborate with? The silos in education run across disciplines. Instructional staff are many and varied within a school environment. From speech–language pathologists, related arts teachers, and instructional coaches to instructional assistants, librarians, and counselors, forming partnerships with key school staff can help your teachers to overcome challenges that otherwise may come to you. With training, silos can be dismantled and partnerships enhanced in ways that benefit the learner and the teacher. While lack of training in how to participate as a member of an effective team was uncovered in Chapter 4, this chapter addresses another reason for the lack of effective collaboration and the resulting silos in education – poor or nonexistent systems thinking among individuals and teams.

The elementary school IEP team had already met four times trying to agree on the proposed IEP. Delonte was a fifth-grade student with Autism Spectrum Disorder (ASD) and the family sought legal counsel due to the extent of difficulty Delonte was having during distance learning. The initial IEP that was developed, according to the lawyer, failed to capture the needs that Delonte was showing now. In order to engage in online class successfully, the family needed to be with him every minute. And as a result, the family felt that the team should consider a regionalized program designed for students with ASD. As the team reviewed the draft IEP, page by page, support by support, the lawyer would come back with a question or a comment that made it clear the team was operating within silos. Things that should be connected were not. Repeatedly, she would challenge the group to look at the big picture as it related to Delonte's school experience. "Why are you saying he needs a reading intervention? On page seven, you reported that he had achieved his grade-level goal in reading. Is he on grade-level? Why are the data saying two different things?" Each time this happened, the team would fall silent. Good question. Why did we say it like that? "Delonte is a whole person," his mother would remind us. "He needs this help all the time, not just when he goes to the SLP." This parent and advocate pushed the team to think about Delonte's needs through a more personal perspective rather than through the isolated bits of information that we gather to measure progress. It was a valuable lesson for the team. If the team had been addressing the whole child in an integrated manner, it was not communicated to the family as such.

The fields of implementation science and systems change challenge us to think about change and growth through a systems perspective. Systems change is a way of thinking about a situation that helps us look for and at the interconnected root cause of problems so that we can determine the best steps to take while accounting for the interconnections within and without the system. Basically, we step back and see the student, teacher, and school staff through a perspective that recognizes that we are not one thing, we are many. A student who struggles with reading in a small group is also a student trying to learn in the whole group and across multiple contents. He is a member of the third grade. He is a member of the school. He is a child, sibling, and a friend. He is a part of a community, church, and extended family. This child's reading difficulties may impact his success within many systems. For Delonte, his disability was affecting his relationship at home with his parent and his ability to access the curriculum. The IEP team had identified that he needed a reading intervention, speech therapy, occupational therapy, and social skills training. He was receiving all of these. If he was not part of larger systems that were impacted by his disability, the solutions the team had put into place for him might have been sufficient, at least in the sense that he was receiving support for isolated skill development. Delonte's disability in autism, however, impacted him across settings both at school and at home. The IEP team, in problem-solving, failed to connect his services to the bigger picture for this student, and the lawyer made this clear.

    I am regularly called by speech-language pathologists, teachers, IEP facilitators, and administrators to help resolve an issue that has arisen. My support always sounds the same. As a matter of fact, I have taken to saying before I respond, "You know I'm a broken record with this, but let's talk about why this is happening." The context, or system, that the student or educator exists within is always important and relevant to the solution or response. You cannot rely on one-size-fits-all policies to solve most problems. Generally, these policies provide a framework to understand "a" system, but not "the" system. They give us a starting point to begin to understand how to proceed to resolve the conflict. In Delonte's situation, the first steps to overcoming this challenge involved facilitating collaboration of the team members through discussion that uncovered the systems to be addressed so that supports could be aligned.

Systems thinking is needed in teams but also for individuals in education to resolve conflict effectively. I received a call from Jade, a speech-language pathologist at an elementary school. Jade is an exceptional SLP and has embraced collaborative practice with many of her teachers, especially the pre-K teachers. A parent of a pre-K student on her caseload had expressed frustration with the virtual services and had written a letter saying she wanted to discontinue services. Jade was very upset with this. The student, Michael, was at the pre-intentional behavior level (level 1) and emerging into the intentional behavior level (level 2). It was so important for services to continue for this student.

In the letter, the parent claimed that the use of pictures to promote communication was the wrong thing to do and that the school should have been using a voice output communication system instead. Additionally, the school was not even providing enough services, according to the parent. Jade explained to me that because the student was at the pre-intentional level and was prone to throwing things, it was not the right time for expensive complex voice output systems. She also explained that she and the special education teacher were working on communication together. He basically was being supported every day to learn to communicate. Jade's frustration was clear. She didn't understand why this was happening and felt attacked by the parent.

I approached this problem through a systems-thinking perspective. From a siloed perspective, Jade was correct. The current recommendations for communication support were appropriate. From a systems approach, there were additional perspectives that had not been accounted for sufficiently. The solution required the team to consider additional information. My conversation was framed by a series of questions that helped to uncover important systems that wrap around this student and family and influence the parent's perspective. My questions also helped to uncover professional systems which could be impacting the understanding of speech therapy services. My conversation sounded like this:

- Why do you think the parent wants a voice output system?

- In what ways have you looped in the augmentative and alternative communication (AAC) specialist?

- Is the family working with a hospital or clinic for speech therapy services?

- Are you familiar with the research on AAC for children in the pre-intentional stage of development?

- Has the team discussed the parent's concerns at an IEP meeting?

- Have you held a parent/teacher conference this school year?

- How is the family doing with helping the student access online instruction?

- What additional supports do you think this family could receive at home to help with these challenges they are experiencing?

- Do you think the parent understands how communication development will unfold for their child given the extent of the disability?

- How do you think the parent feels about the school system's response to their concerns/ complaints?

Each of these questions opens up different systems and relationships that exist for the student and family and school. For a parent to feel heard, it is important to understand the perspective that they see education from. Our responses, when informed by these perspectives and personally relevant systems, become more aligned to the needs of the whole child, not just isolated components within the difficulties the student is experiencing. After gathering information from the SLP, I called the family to discuss concerns. Nothing changed in the IEP, but we did agree to meet through an IEP meeting to consider some of the recommendations that outside SLPs were suggesting. At the meeting, I took the opportunity to explain our services and supports through the systems perspective of the parent. The parent, while still concerned, felt heard and her frustrations began to ease. If I had said to the parent that our services and recommendations are fine, without placing our recommendations within the context of the challenges this family was experiencing, we would not have so quickly been able to resolve the issue and get services resumed.

In systems thinking, teachers understand the ways in which students learn and the systems that wrap around a student's success.

Our work requires systems thinking and is the most successful when team members have an understanding of that. Change is hard. Adding new strategies and structures to an already busy life is not easy. When teams are trained to understand the change that they, their colleagues, and their students and families are experiencing through a systems-thinking perspective, stress is alleviated.

SYSTEMS THINKING FOR STRUGGLING LEARNERS

I find that many educators have heard of various concepts in education, but only have a rudimentary understanding. When I talk with teams who feel that a student needs to be supported in a more restrictive environment, they are surprised and, honestly, angry that we can't simply move the student to the new classroom or school. Educators who really understand the system they work within will be able to make instructional moves effectively because they understand the responsibility they have to support and protect the rights of the individual learner. When teachers know the differences between Universal Design for Learning (UDL), Response to Intervention (RTI), and Least Restrictive Environment (LRE), they know how to ask for help, who to go to, and where to find appropriate resources.

SYSTEMS THINKING AT THE CLASSROOM LEVEL

As you plan to share these ideas at staff meetings or professional developments, I recommend you invite your teachers and teams to identify a few struggling learners they currently teach. Write a brief description of each student's areas of challenge. Provide teams the opportunity to consider these systems thinking concepts in relationship to the student(s) they have selected.

Universal Design for Learning (UDL)

According to CAST, "Universal Design for Learning is a framework to improve and optimize teaching and learning for all people based on scientific insights into how humans learn." At the heart of UDL, teachers consider three principles of learning as they are planning their lessons. Teachers who utilize the principles of UDL understand they have control over how well their lesson will unfold. The curricular tools that are provided to teachers give the teacher a place to start building their lesson, and then effective teachers look for ways to address the predictable barriers that will be evident in the diverse classrooms of the twenty-first century. Lessons should be planned with the three UDL principles embedded.

1. The "Why" of Learning: Engagement

    a. The Engagement principle asks teachers to consider that "learners differ markedly in the ways in which they can be engaged or motivated to learn." Understanding this, teachers can use the Engagement UDL Guidelines as a resource to discover effective means to address student engagement. Teachers will find tools to help recruit interest, sustain effort and persistence, and support self-regulation.

2. The "What" of Learning: Representation

    a. The Representation principle asks teachers to consider that "learners differ in the ways that they perceive and comprehend information that is presented to them." Understanding this, teachers can use the Representation UDL Guidelines as a resource to discover effective ways to address representation. Teachers will find tools to help minimize the impact of perception differences that occur due to auditory or visual impairments, difficulties with language and symbols, and comprehension challenges.

3. The "How" of Learning: Action and Expression

   a. The Action and Expression principle asks teachers to consider that "learners differ in ways that they can navigate a learning environment and express what they know." Understanding this, teachers can use the Action and Expression UDL Guidelines as a resource to discover effective ways to address expression. Teachers will find tools to help support physical action, expression and communication, and executive functions.

Who holds primary responsibility? Classroom Teacher, Inclusion Special Education Teacher
Who might be helpful team members? Grade-Level Team Members, Instructional Resource Teachers/Coaches, Counselors
Where can I find resources to help me understand better?
https://www.cast.org/impact/universal-design-for-learning-udl

Response to Intervention (RTI)

According to the RTI Action Network, "Response to Intervention (RTI) is a multi-tiered approach to help struggling learners. Students' progress is closely monitored at each stage of intervention to determine the need for further research-based instruction and/or intervention in general education, in special education, or both." At the heart of RTI is a belief that the majority of students who struggle can actually be supported with adjustments in the general education classroom environment at Tier 1. Teachers implement supports, and through progress monitoring, students are recommended for progressively more intensive supports in Tier 2 and Tier 3. This team-based approach utilizes the UDL principles as well as intervention models to help students without waiting for them to fail so that IEP eligibility can be considered.

1. Tier 1: High-Quality Classroom Instruction, Screening, and Group Interventions

> a. Teachers develop lessons utilizing high-quality, scientifically based instructional resources and models. Universal Design for Learning is embedded within the Tier 1 instructional model.
> b. Students are screened periodically, whether formally or informally, to determine if academic or behavioral supports are needed.
> c. Teachers seek help to identify effective instructional strategies and keep data to track the impact of the strategy on struggling students.

Who holds primary responsibility? Classroom Teacher, Inclusion Special Education Teacher.
Who might be helpful team members? Grade-Level Team Members, Instructional Resource Teachers/Coaches, Counselors, Speech-Language Pathologists.
Where can I find resources to help me understand better?
http://www.rtinetwork.org/learn/what/whatisrti
https://www.cast.org/impact/universal-design-for-learning-udl

2. Tier 2: Targeted Interventions

   a. Utilizing data collected in Tier 1, teachers identify additional supports. Considerations include group size, frequency, and duration of intervention.
   b. Selected supports are provided in addition to the instruction in the general education classroom and data is kept to track the impact of the intervention.

Who holds primary responsibility? Classroom Teacher, Inclusion Special Education Teacher.
Who might be helpful team members? Grade-Level Team Members, Instructional Resource Teachers/Coaches, Counselors, Speech-Language Pathologists, Interventionists, Psychologists.
Where can I find resources to help me understand better?
http://www.rtinetwork.org/learn/what/whatisrti
https://www.cast.org/impact/universal-design-for-learning-udl
https://ies.ed.gov/ncee/wwc/PracticeGuides

3. Tier 3: Intensive Interventions and Comprehensive Evaluation

   a. Utilizing data collected in Tier 2, teams identify intensive, individualized interventions.
   b. Data is collected to determine impact of intervention and potentially used for referral to special education.

Who holds primary responsibility? Classroom Teacher, Inclusion Special Education Teacher, Interventionist(s).
Who might be helpful team members? Grade-Level Team Members, Instructional Resource Teachers/Coaches, Counselors, Speech-Language Pathologists, Interventionists, Psychologists.
Where can I find resources to help me understand better?
http://www.rtinetwork.org/learn/what/whatisrti

https://www.cast.org/impact/universal-design-for-learning-udl
https://ies.ed.gov/ncee/wwc/PracticeGuides
https://ies.ed.gov/ncee/wwc/FWW

Least Restrictive Environment (LRE)

According to the IRIS Center Peabody College Vanderbilt University, "Least restrictive environment (LRE) is a guiding principle in the Individuals with Disabilities Education Act (IDEA). IDEA necessitates that

- students with disabilities receive their education alongside their peers without disabilities to the maximum extent appropriate and

- students should not be removed from the general education classroom unless learning cannot be achieved even with the use of supplementary aids and services."

This principle within the law can create high levels of frustration and stress for teachers, administrators, and parents when it is not properly understood. Before the seventies, students with disabilities did not have access to school or same-age peers. Parents were often left to instruct these children without support and at their own expense. Parents lobbied congress resulting in a series of landmark legislative actions giving students with disabilities access to instruction in their home schools and with same-age peers. When students are recommended for special education supports, teachers are often surprised that after months of struggling with a student, they find that the student will be staying in their classroom and the teacher must accommodate instruction for the student. The UDL practices and small group instruction written into IEPs become requirements protected by the legal safeguards of IDEA. Students, when given services and supports, should be able to receive/experience the following, as IDEA states:

1. Make progress toward meeting identified academic or functional annual goals.

2. Be involved and make progress in the general education curriculum, as well as to participate in extracurricular (e.g., drama club) and other nonacademic (e.g., a school football game) activities.

3. Take part in these activities with other students, both with and without disabilities.

Who holds primary responsibility? **All** IEP Team Members share responsibility.
Who might be helpful team members? Grade-Level Team Members, Instructional Resource Teachers/Coaches, Counselors, Speech-Language Pathologists, Psychologists.
Where can I find resources to help me understand better?
https://iris.peabody.vanderbilt.edu/wp-content/uploads/pdf_info_briefs/IRIS_Least_Restrictive_Environment_InfoBrief_092519.pdf

SYSTEMS THINKING AT THE STUDENT LEVEL

In Jade's situation earlier, her attempt to resolve a conflict was hindered by the siloed lens she viewed the problem through. From this perspective, she was right, but when considered through the lens of the parent or an outside professional, there were aspects of her recommendation that did not line up. As with the "Systems Thinking at the Classroom Level," it is helpful for you and your teachers to consider the information below with a specific student in mind as you discuss the following questions.

Academic Achievement

1. Student System: What is the specific area of difficulty the student demonstrates? (e.g., difficulties in reading, math or writing, comprehension or speaking, following directions or attending to instruction) How does this impact the student personally? In comparison to peers, does the student have control over decisions?

2. Classroom System: How does the student engage in academics across all content areas? How do the student's areas of difficulty impact their participation and success in academics across all content areas?

3. School System: How does the student engage academically (show up academically) in relation to the larger school as a system? How do the student's areas of difficulty impact their participation in school routines, school celebrations, school trips, or use of resources (e.g., SLP, counselor, administrator, etc.)?

Nonacademic Achievement

1. Student System: How does the student's area of difficulty impact the student personally during lunch, recess, and other nonacademic times? Does the student have friendships? Is

the student bullied? Does the student bully? Does the student transition between activities effectively? How is his attendance? How does he do on the bus?

2. Classroom System: How do the student's areas of difficulty impact their participation and success in nonacademic areas across all contents?

3. School System: How does the student engage nonacademically (show up nonacademically) in relation to the larger school as a system? How do the student's areas of difficulty impact their participation in school routines, school celebrations, school trips, or use of resources (e.g., SLP, counselor, administrator, etc.)?

Home Perspective

1. How do the student's parents see his/her academic strengths and needs at home? What are the concerns of the parent for the student individually, in the classroom, and in the school?

2. Are there concerns for the student in the community (e.g., at the playground, at the store, etc.)?

3. Have the parents received additional information from a hospital or clinic?

4. Are there health issues that complicate this student's life?

5. Does the family have sufficient resources to help the student at home?

6. What are the competing demands of the household that could impact a parent's ability to help?

After considering the student through the systems thinking perspective of individual, classroom, school, and home, consider a solution to address the area of concern you stated for the student. As a team, discuss if your solution addresses the actual need presented by the area of difficulty.

- Academic and Nonacademic

- Individual, Class, and School Level

- Home Concerns

In the case of Delonte, a systems thinking perspective would have afforded the team an opportunity to present a more unified explanation of the services and supports while recognizing the need for individualized services across multiple areas of development. Decision-making for Delonte would require considerations of UDL and LRE, student growth in academic and nonacademic areas, and parental concerns regarding access to education through a virtual format. An additional benefit of systems thinking is that it offers teams a way to predict the challenges that lawyers and advocates will present teams like those in Delonte's case.

Systems thinking places students, teachers, parents, and the work of the classroom within a systems context. Solving student problems requires teachers to reflect on the level in which the problem exists and the systems that are contributing factors that could impede progress. I have found that when teams and individuals think about problems from the big picture lens, they often find more comprehensive and appropriate solutions. I encourage you to invest time to strengthen your staff's skills in systems thinking.

These key foundational principles and priorities are where I spend a good deal of time when I'm helping teams resolve problems — helping teachers and education teams simply understand the landscape they are working in. If this sounds like a lot and more than teachers can manage, I understand. The next two chapters will help clarify how a teacher is supposed to effectively do all of this.

PERSPECTIVE 3 – THE DIVERSE CLASSROOM

Up until this point, we have focused solely on the difficulties and challenges of the struggling learner. It is time to consider the whole child! Peter Senge in *Schools That Learn* tells us that when we only look at a child through the label of deficits and delays, "[e]ventually, the labels take over."

Andrew was a third-grade student. His family hired an attorney to help them advocate for Andrew as the IEP team was considering eligibility for the second time. Andrew struggled with school anxiety and had met regularly with the school counselor for two years. His parents had asked for him to be tested in second grade despite the team's disagreement that this was necessary. He was reading on grade level and doing fine in math. The testing that was completed basically supported this and he was not found eligible for special education. Despite this outcome, his parents continued to ask for help for him. He had a hard time focusing, spelling was difficult, and recalling what he had learned was next to impossible for him. His parents communicated with his teacher every day. This was too much for his teacher. She felt attacked by the parents and disrespected. She was, after all, the teacher. What does a parent know about the learning happening in the classroom? In third grade and with a strained relationship with the school, they asked again for help from special education. This time, the parents went to an outside examiner and had Andrew tested. This time, the testing showed a disability.

I worked with the Director of Compliance and the IEP team to develop an IEP based on the assessment results, classroom data, and parent concerns. By the time the IEP was finished, everyone was thoroughly frustrated. The teacher felt betrayed by the family and let down by the school, the principal felt frustrated that he'd supported his teacher only to find out more could have been done to help this student, the parent was angry that every step of the way was an uphill battle to help their child, and the student was becoming embarrassed by the sudden attention in the classroom on top of managing the ongoing anxiety issues. The remedy, a sophisticated system of supports that required the expertise and dedication of a team of professionals, quickly resulted in improvements for the student, and a relationship of trust between school and home began to emerge.

This sophisticated program was written within Andrew's IEP, but the majority of the supports could have been provided, if the teacher and educational team knew, without an IEP. Researchers tell us about the hidden curriculum that exists within a classroom. Each teacher has his or her own set of expectations and students often have to figure out what those are by trial and error. Andrew, however, was not a student who could easily pick up the unspoken rules and follow them. Instead, he struggled to learn and fit in with peers and ultimately needed help from the school counselor. Students with disabilities, like Andrew, and those from diverse backgrounds are often more impacted by this hidden curriculum than students not from marginalized groups or communities.

In years of helping teachers see the inherent barriers that exist within their classrooms, I have become keenly aware that this same concept exists for teachers. There is a hidden curriculum within the educational system, aspects of learning that are lightly brushed upon in training and rarely ever given sufficient attention beyond teacher preparation programs. Not only is limited time given to understanding how our educational system is organized, but there are strong beliefs that surround many of the core principles. *Parents should do more to prepare students. Students should complete homework at home. Students should listen to teachers. Teachers teach the curriculum, not behavior. Teachers should not pressure my child. Students with disabilities don't belong here. Students with behavior issues should not be allowed in my school.* The list goes on and the barriers to teacher and school success are massive.

Years of helping resolve barriers to instruction have illuminated the need for teachers to develop core knowledge around key principles and priorities within the educational system.

ALL LEARNERS ARE LIKE SNOWFLAKES

Students are like snowflakes – each is an individual. Andrew's unique profile of strengths and weaknesses was not like any other general education student in the school. While this familiar analogy points us in a direction to sympathize with the uniqueness of students as individual people, it falls short on helping us understand what we can or should do about it when students begin to struggle. And this is an important difference between successful schools and struggling schools. Schools that do not seek to understand in what ways students are likely to be different often end up in a battle "between us and them" when systems are not in place to address the expected needs of students.

Perspective 3: The Diverse Classroom recognizes that the school is a complex system that was introduced in largely its current format in the early to mid-1900s. While the way we teach and organize schools has not changed significantly over time, the student body we teach has changed enormously. Classrooms today are diverse environments with students from all social and economic backgrounds, racial and ethnic groups, and ability levels. For all the condemnation of the public schools, the diversity of our schools is the very reason I am so proud to work in public education. This is my soapbox! Every day, teachers, SLPs, administrators, instructional assistants, and coaches get to work together to change the opportunity for a child. And when we are really lucky, we get to do this for a student who struggles. I regularly tell anyone and everyone who is within earshot that this is the best work a person could commit their life to.

Perspective 3 is deep and layered with the cries from various social movements. As I discuss it here, however, I would like to bring you to a foundational framework. I believe all people are fundamentally the same. While we are different in lots of ways that make us who we are as a group or an individual, we can start from a point of view that says, "All people can learn," and, "All people have value." From here, I would like to share with you a way of thinking about individual differences through a collective lens.

The classroom is made up of a group of individual learners. Within this group, certain strengths and weaknesses are to be expected. I call this "predictable variability in a learning group." We know that some students will be strong readers. Some students will be average readers. And some students will be struggling readers. For almost all classrooms, this will be true. Because I can predict that there will be a range of reading levels, I can from the beginning prepare my lessons to allow access to every student. This knowledge ties back to resources that would help me develop a UDL-embedded lesson plan. A lesson that has been built for the predictable variation within a normal population set will allow the class to more likely learn the first time and require fewer repetitions through small group instruction.

For reading, most of us are really comfortable with this idea of a variety of levels of readers learning in one classroom. Now, let's consider the full range of development and this idea of predictable variability. In early childhood, there are four primary domains of development – physical, cognitive, social, and emotional. Within each of these areas of development, we can predict that a range of abilities and developmental timelines will emerge. Some students will have exceptional physical skills. Some students will have average physical skills. Some students will have low physical skills. And this same pattern can be seen across all areas of development.

Because this pattern of developmental variability can be predicted, it is valuable for teachers and education team members to consider this perspective as a means to prepare for the needs of their class of students. Where it can become challenging to conceptualize is that any one student can (and will) have strengths in some areas and weaknesses in others and no two students will have the same combination of strengths and weaknesses. Students are like snowflakes – all the same and all different. And while we intuitively know that the variability between individuals exists, our classrooms and school structures are often built for a classroom with less variation. Curriculum resources are designed to help teachers effectively teach agreed-upon standards, and while they are built to provide opportunity for a range of students, they are not built to account for the variation in all learners. All curriculums instruct teachers to differentiate. Some even provide examples of how to differentiate for various groups such as English Learners. When a teacher does not understand the predictability in learner variation, he/ she may end up using ineffective methods to manage student participation to the detriment not only in the learning for the targeted students, but ultimately to the classroom as well.

We are teaching a curricular standard recognizing that not all students possess the prerequisite skills in all domains of development. When teachers can see the student within the curriculum as a system, he/ she will prepare differently, advocate more effectively, and collaborate with parents through a sympathetic lens that understands there is nothing inherently wrong with the child that time, supports, and consistency can't address. In second grade, Andrew was struggling to learn to spell. He probably was not the only student in the classroom with this challenge. The second-grade classroom could be a place that recognizes that needs will arise across the primary domains of development with subsequent UDL strategies embraced to support and ease the discomfort of both the student and the teacher.

When you put these concepts together, curriculum, predictable variability, and domains of development, we begin to see the foundation of the educational landscape. Teaching is more than curriculum, routines, and schedules. Teachers who recognize that they will never have a classroom that is one-size-fits-all are better prepared for the work ahead.

Unpacking the Diverse Classroom

As you plan to share these ideas at staff meetings or professional developments, you may need to explain to the group that it is possible for special education teachers, speech-language pathologists, and others with a specific focus to engage in this activity as well. The variability within their student groups may not be as extreme, but the variability is certainly there.

In groups, consider the following areas of development. What would students look like if their skills were higher than average, average, and lower than average?

Area of Development	Higher Than Average	Average	Lower Than Average
Reading Level: Whole class lesson			
Reading Comprehension Level			
Written Expression: Paragraph level			
Mathematics Level: Problem solving			
Attention			
Emotional Regulation			
Social Skills			

Now consider how you might adjust a lesson or routine to increase the rigor or the access to instruction for the higher than average and lower than average groups.

Area of Development	Higher Than Average	Lower Than Average
Reading Level: Whole class lesson		
Reading Comprehension Level		
Written Expression: Paragraph level		
Mathematics Level: Problem solving		
Attention		
Emotional Regulation		
Social Skills		

It is also important to reflect on your cultural responsiveness in the classroom. Just like with challenges in understanding and preparing for the ability differences that will exist within a classroom, teachers who prepare for the cultural diversity of their classrooms will be able to create an inclusive and equitable climate for their students.

In what ways is cultural and ethnic diversity represented in your class? Consider socioeconomic status, race, English learner, gender, religion.

Predicting that your classroom will be culturally and ethnically diverse, how might you prepare differently?

Sometimes when students struggle or interact differently, teachers and other educators are tempted to say, "The student doesn't belong in this class." UDL, RTI, and LRE help us to understand why students who struggle remain in general education classes. But Perspective 3 helps us look differently at the challenge of helping a room full of snowflakes. We can predict not only that there will be a range of learners in every classroom, but also that students in our classrooms will be needing the support of the RTI process and are protected in their right to be in your class even with a significant disability through LRE provisions. In helping educators, I have seen the reoccurring theme that the answer for the student exists somewhere else with someone else. I'm not sure where the origin of this thinking comes from, but research and legislation do not support these ideas. When teachers and schools hold onto these outdated perspectives, it creates a feeling of helplessness in the teacher. It also robs the teacher of incredible success and happiness in his/her work. It is hard to help students who learn differently, and it is exceptionally hard to help them when we have not planned for, nor accepted, that individuals who learn differently will be in our classrooms. These hard topics, however, are punctuated with the reassuring knowledge that students *do* learn in diverse, inclusive classrooms when they are engineered for the unique student group. And in the process, we show students and families how to create communities that recognize, value, and lift up those who are different and in need of our support.

PERSPECTIVE 4 – EVIDENCE-BASED PRACTICE

I was asked to observe a student in a kindergarten reading class. A parent had emailed the principal about lack of access to instruction for Jason, her child. She said that Ms. Jenkins, the teacher, was refusing to help Jason and as a result, the school was failing her child. On the day of the observation, I arrived a few minutes before the students were to arrive to school for the day. Reading was the first class on the kindergarten schedule. Ms. Jenkins told me to be on the lookout for a Caucasian boy who would run into the classroom every morning. He should be easy to spot since no other student started the day this way. And just as anticipated, a few minutes later, Jason came running into the classroom, with a smile on his face. He dropped his bookbag at the door and ran to the block center, pulling out blocks rapidly. For the next thirty minutes, I watched as the teacher tried to get Jason to follow the class routines. She gave him directives, walked him to his spaces, and tried to engage him in the lesson by asking questions and prompting him to look at pictures in the book she was reading to the class. These efforts were not successful. Jason whined, rolled around on the floor, and spent much of the instructional period looking at and poking other students.

Later that day, when I met with Ms. Jenkins, she said she had tried everything she could think of and was so frustrated. She was upset that the parent had contacted the principal and now he was questioning her, even though she was trying her best to help him. And yes, I could see that she was doing things for him that she was not doing for others. I could also see that what she was doing was not working. When I asked her to tell me what she thought needed to happen, she quickly said that he really doesn't belong in a general education classroom. Her other students were being impacted and she thought the special education teacher needed to do more to help him.

As we looked together at the difficulties the student was experiencing, I used the Four Perspectives to gather information and to help Ms. Jenkins understand that there was more to the situation than she was acknowledging. Helping students like Jason required systematic, deliberate action. Ms. Jenkins needed my help to understand that the least restrictive environment for Jason was her classroom. It may have been true that Jason needed more special education supports, but without a way of knowing if appropriate evidence-based practices had been utilized, we were going to need to start at the beginning of a data-informed cycle. Ms. Jenkins had been trying to help but what she was doing had not been helpful. Was it because of the extent of the disability (as Ms. Jenkins thought) or was it due to how she was teaching him? We needed to figure this out.

I met again with Ms. Jenkins to create a plan. Clearly the morning routine was sabotaging his success in reading. He needed access to a routine with supports. Participation during whole group reading needed more structure and how the student was asked to engage needed more consideration. We chose to start with two evidence-based practices found to be highly effective for students:

pair words with visuals and link abstract concepts to concrete representations.

Ms. Jenkins was relying on lots of spoken words to influence his behavior and to teach him routines and new academic skills. Using the strong evidence-based practice (EBP) of pairing words to visuals to help him more successfully enter the classroom and hang up his bookbag, we created a visual schedule that the kindergarten IA used as he entered the classroom. Paired with a reinforcement system in which he earned time in the block center when he entered the classroom using the visual schedule, the student quickly improved and on most days was following a more traditional model for entering the classroom. Jason's reinforcement system was designed to visually show Jason that he was meeting the expectation of the teacher. When he followed the routine for entering, he would, with the help of his IA, place a smiley sticker on a chart. Earning a smiley sticker was the signal that he could have five minutes in the block center. It also helped Ms. Jenkins collect data on how well Jason was doing over time!

Building on this EBP to further increase the number of successful days, Ms. Jenkins and the IA created a sequence of pictures of Jason's classmates doing this same routine. They met briefly each day with Jason to talk about the pictures and practiced the "entering" routine daily during the day. Jason's success rate soared within two weeks. Ms. Jenkins was able to see the change in a short period of time and was motivated to continue this work. The visual schedule, the picture sequence, and the practice helped the student because of the underlying evidence-based practice that guided the decision-making and interactions of the teacher with Jason. Teachers often rely on ineffective methods because they are not trained to recognize or look for the high impact practice. Using words only to guide and correct behavior works for many students, but when students do not respond, it is important for teachers not to give up. I tell all educators who I help thatone of the best parts of working in education in the twenty-first century is the access to research that helps me to be effective.

When students struggle with reading, we often hear solutions from teachers like, "I changed the reading level and he's still struggling," "I gave him a different worksheet," or, "I explained it again to him and he still isn't getting it." Of course, by the time I'm involved in helping, teachers have experienced lots of failure and are frustrated, so the responses are often defensive and angry. Teachers recognize when students are struggling, and they try to help them in the ways they know how. Sadly, most teachers do not speak the language of evidence-based practice. As a matter of fact, this concept, EBP, is often a dirty word in education. It is thrown around as the answer, yet few actually connect the solutions to the practices that we know change the trajectory of learning for students.

Undergraduate programs expose preservice teachers to key methodologies, but not at a level that drives discussion and decision-making at the school level. When was the last time you had a teacher come to you and say that they added ten minutes of discussion to each lesson and have seen ten out of thirteen struggling students improve in comprehension? That they are going to meet with the three students who are still struggling to give them ten more minutes of discussion? I suspect never. This is an EBP beneficial for adolescent students in language arts. Most teachers will say they can't sacrifice time for discussion. Yet, discussion is a practice that teachers could or should consider based on research. Have you ever had a teacher come to you saying, "I need help to connect the abstract concepts to concrete representations for students in my class?" Again, most likely you have not heard requests for help like this. Teachers give struggling students more time, send work home to complete for homework, reduce the number of items a student completes, tell them to work harder and stay focused, and maybe even give the student the answer. And if it is a student with behavior issues, the repertoire of strategies is just as limited and ineffective as for those with academic challenges. Yet, as we discussed in Chapter 6, we can predict that we will have all types of students with all types of needs, so having an arsenal of EBPs that truly work is not optional.

When principals and education leaders communicate about students through an EBP framework, we move students systematically to increasingly more and more successful states. EBPs that a teacher implements within a general education or special education classroom are not the only supports that schools provide, but they should be the starting point for supports.

When some teachers come to administrators for help, they make a case that there is nothing more they can do. The student is the problem and the administrator needs to do something about it. As teachers explain all of the things they have done to help the student, it can be difficult to tease out fact from opinion. With all of the acronyms and support systems available to students, communicating about supports for students can be quite confusing. It can sound very convincing that there is nothing more a teacher can do.

I was asked by a principal to attend a Student Support Team (SST) meeting for an English learner. This student was a native Spanish speaker who received ESOL support and had been placed in an intervention for reading. The SST team wanted to refer the student to the IEP team for testing because the student was not making sufficient progress. The team had work samples, intervention data, and analysis of performance over time. It looked obvious that all that could be done was done and a referral to special education was the right thing to do for this struggling student. But, this was not the case. The intervention did not address phonological awareness deficits or sound system differences in the native Spanish speaker. Some responses noted as errors were actually dialectal variation. When you look at supports through a curricular lens, the solution seemed to be the right fit and the rationale that the problem was within the student seemed reasonable. This one perspective on why the student was struggling did not offer enough clarity to really determine if it was reasonable to suspect a disability.

The team argued that they had given the student a reading intervention in a small group three times a week, and the student did not make any progress. When you look at the student's needs through an EBP lens, however, you see a different story. The student was not progressing because of underlying skill deficits (or delays due to learning a second language). If we asked, how can I connect the abstract (phonics) to the concrete (her sound system), our intervention would have been different. This student's progress would likely have been observed more quickly. When we skip steps in the developmental pathway for learning, we slow learning down significantly and maybe even create disability. Using an EBP approach also allows for repeated iterations of support that can naturally lead to the conclusion that special education is the right next step all the while helping the student to learn.

The educational environment is a noisy place – both literally and figuratively. Figuratively, teachers are asked to implement new programs every year, participate in grant activities specifically tailored to their class or a small group, participate in community-building activities like award ceremonies, after school groups, and fundraisers, and engage in book studies around a hot topic, all while managing the typical responsibilities associated with teaching. It is reasonable to see that teachers may not know of or seek out evidence-based practices related to their classrooms.

The challenge is amplified by the fact that no one else in the school talks like this. Communication about student needs is often centered around poorly implemented support systems, SST meetings that do not require a rigorous accounting of what was tried, and complaints that no one is helping them. This last statement is heard from every instructional group, not just teachers. We do not have a culture of communication centered on EBPs despite the resounding research that tells us which practices to prioritize.

It's not what you do, but why you do it. For example, there are many ways to teach a child to read. As a matter of fact, the ongoing dispute about reading pedagogy keeps districts and lawmakers in almost constant discussion about why students are not learning to read in the US. And while a whole language approach can work for some students, a structured phonics-based approach is the only way that works for others. The key decision-making practices within these approaches are the true sources of magic that allow for reading acquisition to actually occur.

I was assigned to help teachers who had been trained to implement the Wilson Reading Program. Select teachers and reading coaches had attended a three-day intensive training to learn the program. Then over the course of five months, each participant received one day of coaching by a certified trainer. The coach would observe an intervention session then meet with the teacher for an hour going over the session and helping them plan for the next lesson. By the end of the school year, we had highly trained interventionists, or so we thought. This one practice that I've mentioned a few times already – connecting the abstract to concrete – turns out to be a key practice when helping students in a program like a Tier 3 reading intervention. Teachers have to see the error within the developmental level that the student understands (this is what is concrete for the student) and then connect this to the new learning (the abstract). Some teachers understood that while they might be saying, "This is a CVC shape," that actually those words acted as the scaffold between where the student was and where they needed him or her to go. Teachers who did not have this foundational EBP understanding simply said the words, but missed the nuanced adjustments needed to make it relevant to each student in the group. And, as I'm sure you already know, the students did not progress as expected in the intervention.

Unpacking Evidence-Based Practice

One of the greatest barriers to use of EBPs that I have observed is that we currently do not have a culture of EBP in our schools. By this I mean, we don't use the language of EBP. As you seek to increase the competency of your staff to solve problems through an EBP perspective, you must first provide guidance as to which practices teachers should focus their attention on. There are many practices, but not all will result in the fastest growth for students. I want our teachers and schools to see the benefit of their efforts quickly, so selection of which EBP is critically important.

I will discuss which practices are not negotiable that all teachers must know. I will also show you where you can find resources to help you bring these tools to your teachers.

Institute for Education Sciences (IES) Practice Guides

- https://ies.ed.gov/ncee/wwc/PracticeGuides

The Institute for Education Sciences is an organization funded by your tax dollars. It was specifically created to make the dissemination of best practices easily accessible for educators. According to the IES, "A practice guide is a publication that presents recommendations for educators to address challenges in their classrooms and schools. They are based on reviews of research, the experiences of practitioners, and the expert opinions of a panel of nationally recognized experts." There are currently twenty-four practice guides. Within these, I return over and over just a few that represent the basic knowledge all teachers need to obtain related to EBP.

Organizing Instruction and Study to Improve Student Learning – This guide contains "some of the most important principles to emerge from research on learning and memory in mind."

a. Space learning over time

b. Interleave worked example solutions with problem-solving exercises

c. Combine graphics with verbal descriptions

d. Connect and integrate abstract and concrete representations of concepts

e. Use quizzing to promote learning

   i. Use pre-questions to introduce a new topic
   ii. Use quizzes to re-expose students to key content

f. Help students allocate study time efficiently

   i. Teach students how to use delayed judgments of learning to identify content that needs further study
   ii. Use tests and quizzes to identify content that needs to be learned

g. Ask deep explanatory questions

    This practice guide has been recognized as one of the most important collections of evidence-based practices for all teachers. The National Council of Teacher Quality, while controversial in their methods of expression, highlighted six of these practices as crucial. They argued that teachers are not adequately prepared in their university programs to understand and use these practices effectively. NCTQ's six strategies that work are: (1) pairing graphics with words, (2) linking abstract concepts with concrete representations, (3) posing probing questions, (4) repeatedly alternating problems with their solutions provided and problems that students must solve, (5) distributing practice and (6) assessing to boost retention.

Ulrich Boser of The Learning Agency also wrote about these key practices in *Learn Better*. The message is that teachers need more time learning about, using, and communicating through these effective practices, from the start.

Reducing Behavior Problems in the Elementary School Classroom

a. Identify the specifics of the problem behavior and the conditions that prompt and reinforce it.

b. Modify the classroom learning environment to decrease problem behavior.

c. Teach and reinforce new skills to increase appropriate behavior and preserve a positive climate.

d. Draw on relationships with professional colleagues and students' families for continued guidance and support.

e. Assess whether schoolwide behavior problems warrant adopting schoolwide strategies or programs.

Visible Learning, John Hattie

- https://visible-learning.org/

Hattie conducted meta-analyses of various evidence-based practices. "Hattie points out that in education most things work. The questions is which ones work best and where to concentrate our efforts." Through his book and website, Hattie visually shows the strength of a given practice thereby encouraging educators to deliberately select and invest time in learning and applying only the strongest practices. From Hattie's "252 Influences and Effect Sizes" graphic, below are the top ten practices that he has found to influence student achievement.

a. Collective teacher efficacy

b. Self-reported grades

c. Teacher estimates of achievement

d. Cognitive task analysis

e. Response to intervention

f. Piagetian programs

g. Jigsaw method

h. Conceptual change programs

i. Prior ability

j. Strategy to integrate with prior knowledge

There are many places you can find strong evidence-based practices, and this is part of the challenge you face. Sifting through the massive amount of information to see the most critical content is daunting. The two sources I list are simply starting points that help focus us on the most important building blocks for successful teaching. With these foundational supports, schools can develop a culture of EBP use through training, discussion, focused/supported application, and ongoing expectations by leadership and within high-performing teams who hold each other accountable.

When I speak to any group, I always ground the discussion in EBPs and where to find them. When I wrote a proposal to increase the supports for new teachers so that they can have more success with behavior/classroom management, my proposal was couched in EBPs. My proposal launched consideration of various programs and ultimately one was selected. And while this is an important first step toward helping teachers improve their classroom management skills, it is not ultimately the program that makes the difference. It is the underlying teaching practices that teachers learn and skillfully use.

Many of the challenges your teachers bring you stem from a lack of preparation of teachers to address the individual needs of students. Having a deep understanding of how to approach supports for students will reduce the number of calls for help to you. And in the process, results in teachers who experience professional success and a sense of control over the needs of his/her students.

FOUR PERSPECTIVES CULTURE

The Four Perspectives I've outlined in Chapters 4 to 7 represent a mindset shift that is supported with tools and practices to help you bring about this level of understanding with your teachers. Some people and teams seem to naturally understand and embrace this way of understanding problems. Like me, they see problems as opportunities to help. For many, however, getting to the heart of the problem is fiendishly difficult and so the Four Perspectives provides a framework to help bridge the gap.

Teachers and education team members need the opportunity to use their creative talents when solving problems. When well-intentioned researchers, publishers, and education leaders put restrictive parameters around solving problems, sometimes we find that our teams simply walk through the motions, just as in the Wilson Reading Program training examples shared in Chapter 7.

The Four Perspectives challenges the notion that someone else has all of the answers for students within a classroom or school. When teachers are adequately prepared to unpack complex problems by understanding through the Four Perspectives, they are more likely to identify options that include actual root causes for the student's difficulty and allow for instructional and environmental solutions to appropriately match the true extent of the need.

Additionally, when teachers have a framework to guide collaboration, relationships between team members take on a model for growth that is self-sustaining. One success encourages another attempt, and with each successive success, teams move closer to the most notable EBP, collective teacher efficacy. John Hattie, in *Visible Learning*, through reviews of research on collaboration found that schools that promote actions that result in successes for teachers and students have the building blocks for the high efficacy practice called collective teacher efficacy. As your teachers learn to understand the barriers to success in student achievement and access, they will be better able to adjust instruction and select interventions to meet the root cause needs of struggling learners. Teaching with the Four Perspectives offers an avenue to schoolwide and individual success.

For the education leader who is starting this work without the benefit of an experienced team leader, this chapter provides recommendations for training in, support for, and monitoring of the Four Perspectives. This is systems change work and so a plan for facilitating change will lead to the greatest improvement over time.

FOUR PERSPECTIVES: TRAINING CONSIDERATIONS

Four Perspectives
A Framework to Resolve Challenges for Struggling Learners

Perspective 1: **Effective Teams**	Perspective 2: **Systems Thinking**
Step 1: Form a Team ❏ Who has an understanding of the problem? ❏ Who can help identify a solution in this area? Step 2: Develop Core Competencies ❏ Team Value and Ethics ❏ Interprofessional Communication ❏ Team Expectations and Goals ❏ Using Data Cycles	Step 1: Consider systems impacted by this problem. ❏ For the student ❏ For the classroom ❏ For the school ❏ For the home/community Step 2: Consider how the student's difficulties are helped or hindered by the educational environment. ❏ Academic and nonacademic areas ❏ Instructional frameworks (e.g., UDL, RTI, LRE) ❏ Non-school environments (e.g., home, store)
Perspective 3: **The Diverse Classroom**	Perspective 4: **Evidence-Based Practice**
Determine additional characteristics present in the student and the student's educational environments. ❏ Domains of development ❏ Presence of disability ❏ Cultural considerations	Select a high-impact evidence-based practice Consider: ❏ Pairing graphics with words ❏ Linking abstract concepts with concrete representations ❏ Posing probing questions ❏ Repeatedly alternating solved and unsolved problems ❏ Distributing practice ❏ Assessing to boost retention

"About 20 percent of people and organizations are ready for change at any given time," according to research reported through the Active Implementation Hub. Awareness that your teachers will need you to develop a clear plan for implementation is an important step in the process of bringing the Four Perspectives to your school. As you develop a plan to bring this new information to your school, there are two models I recommend you consider: (1) intensive two-day training with full-year implementation plan or (2) monthly training with a phased one-plus year implementation plan.

Intensive Two-Day Training with Full-Year Implementation

1. Training: Learning about the Four Perspectives

Initial training in the Four Perspectives will be needed to provide your teachers and education team members with the background knowledge needed to begin use of the Four Perspectives framework. The training would both inform and provide an opportunity for participants to experience the Four Perspectives in relationship to current or previous challenges. The Four Perspectives should be unpacked in four half-day sessions. Many of the concepts will be familiar. In these half-day sessions, teachers will reflect, develop a common language, and apply the knowledge/skills to solve challenges presented by struggling students.

Make-Up of Initial Teams

Prior to the training, I recommend that you identify initial teams of three to five members. Be certain to select diverse voices for each team. An ideal team might have two fifth-grade teachers, a behavior specialist, and a special education teacher. Another example might be a first-grade teacher, a literacy teacher, a counselor, and a music teacher. We want to bring together a variety of voices so that teams can experience what it feels like to come together when observable differences in individual preparation (e.g., counselors are trained in different content than teachers) are evident.

Resources

This book can be used as a guide to help you lead your teams to understanding the Four Perspectives. You can use my examples of how I came to recognize each perspective, or you can identify examples from your own experiences or that of your school. Within Chapters 4-7, there are ideas for questions and discussions your teachers will engage with to uncover how the perspective impacts their understanding of problem-solving.

2. Application: Using the Four Perspectives

Teams will set goals to use the Four Perspectives to support problem solving for struggling students. Quarterly, you should meet with all teams to share examples, progress, and difficulties. At this time, teams will adjust their implementation goals. Ideally, you will meet with your teachers to review their progress at least four times during the year.

3. Monitoring: Determining the Impact of the Four Perspectives

As the school principal, you want to see your teachers have greater success solving problems at the classroom level with a reduction in the number of student cases you need to get involved in. To support this objective, I recommend you set two goals. First, a goal for you. When teachers ask for help, use the language of the Four Perspectives. Ask questions through the lens of the Four Perspectives. This will be a process of learning for you as well. Second, track the number of problems that come to you without a solution. You can expect that teachers will continue to need your guidance, but the situation should shift to one of presenting solutions and asking for permission to engage in that solution, rather than simply throwing their hands up in utter frustration.

Monthly Training with Phased One-Plus Year Implementation

1. Training and Application: Learning about and using the Four Perspectives

2. Duration/Frequency: One-hour monthly training.

In a monthly training model, you break the Four Perspectives into bite-size pieces.

Month 1: Introduction to The Diverse Classroom and Systems Thinking

Month 2: Introduction to Evidence-Based Practice

Month 3: Introduction to Effective Teams

Month 4: Introduction to Four Perspectives when Problem Solving

Month 5: Going deeper with The Diverse Classroom and Systems Thinking

Month 6: Going deeper with Evidence-Based Practice and Effective Teams

Month 7: Goal setting and application of Four Perspectives when Problem Solving

Month 8: Reflection and goal setting for continued use of Four Perspectives

Month 9: Intensive one-day training to build and support understanding of Four Perspectives

3. Monitoring: Determining the impact of the Four Perspectives

As with the Intensive two-day model, I recommend you develop goals to monitor the implementation of this work. By Month 4, your teachers will have been provided an introduction to the Four Perspectives and we can begin to encourage them to begin incorporating this mindset in their problem solving, recognizing that until teachers have received full training, our effectiveness data is not reliable. Beginning to collect data early provides guidance for you as you plan each month's training. This way, we can adjust instruction to match the needs of your teachers.

I am confident that your teachers possess the knowledge to solve problems and with a deeper understanding of the educational landscape, they will. The Four Perspectives offer clarity on the terrain of the educational landscape and a road map to yours and their success.

As you develop your staff's understanding of the Four Perspectives, there are some advanced level systems thinking concepts that may help you to consider. These concepts take us to a deeper level of understanding why teachers struggle. In Chapter 5, we considered systems thinking for the classroom and systems thinking for the student. Advanced level systems thinking takes us to the school level and includes three concepts: the translation gap, stages of change, and implementation drivers.

SYSTEMS THINKING AT THE SCHOOL LEVEL

The Translation Gap

A familiar refrain sung by many education leaders is, "Why don't they know this?" It comes as a surprise to new leaders who have just left a successful career in the classroom that many educators are not using effective practices. "How can this be? We did a training in September on how to create learning communities. I saw one classroom using the tools we gave them." This is quite predictable and something that all initiatives are at risk of experiencing. Two lines of research help to inform why this happens. First is research on the translation gap. It can take seventeen years from the time a practice is shown to be effective for its use to emerge within a school setting. Second is the research on the effect of the implementation team. Initiatives that include an implementation team can find that 80 percent of teachers are implementing new practices successfully within three years. Without an implementation team, 14 percent are implementing within seventeen years. Bringing new practices into the educational landscape is a challenge and teaching teams should know this. When teachers understand quantifiably the impact of teams on their change process, they are more likely to welcome the opportunity to engage in this activity.

Stages of Change (National Implementation Research Network)

As teams organize to try new strategies and solutions for students, they are at risk of stopping the strategy too soon. The stages of change help us to understand that we as a team and as individuals move through stages predictably. We first consider the change in the exploration stage, and we prepare by gathering resources and setting expectations in the installation stage.

We initiate the new strategy or structure and then, over time, the new method becomes the way we do business. For larger scale change projects, the entire stages of change can take two to four years to complete. While this is not necessarily true for problem-solving for individual students the stages are still the same. We all want solutions to immediately be put into place. This is not always possible or appropriate given the situation.

Implementation Drivers

You've selected your EBP, your team has agreed to help, and you are off and running only to discover that the new method fails before it's even gotten off the ground. What happened? As we talked about earlier, barriers to success in education are extensive. Rather than throw the baby out with the bathwater, teams should use the implementation drivers to determine if barriers to their efforts can be removed. For example, maybe a teacher needs more training on how to use a practice. Maybe coaching in the classroom is needed. Maybe a step-by-step how-to guide could help the teacher implement the practice better. The implementation drivers offer ways that teams can think about implementation.

These concepts can be developed with the help of implementation science training modules available without cost through the National Implementation Research Network (NIRN). As education leaders use these concepts to support and drive change, teachers become better equipped to meaningfully engage in systems thinking and effective problem-solving.

BARRIERS TO INNOVATION

I have been happily working in education for more than twenty years. Early in my career, Lynn, the Director of Compliance who oversaw the speech-language pathologists, learned that I was teaching an undergraduate course in special education at the local college. She was pleased that I was engaging in this work, in part because she valued my skillset, but largely because she recognized the great disconnect between what new teachers think education is and what education really is and demands of them. She believed that preservice teachers needed to be taught by individuals currently teaching and working in the field as this gave an opportunity for the theories and strategies to be understood through a real-world lens. Lynn valued the contribution of public education to the learning opportunities in higher education. This was a new idea to me. I had always believed without question in the rightness of my professors and the articles I devoured written by researchers in speech-language pathology and education. It was second nature to believe that the challenges I faced were because education was not doing it the way that higher ed and research said it should be. And while I still put great value on the guidance we receive from these groups, I now know with much clarity that it is not enough to know that these answers are out there. How do we bring this knowledge to the schools? How do we help our instructional teams to use the best and strongest practices to help students?

Implementing effective practices like the Four Perspectives framework is hard work, but not for the reasons that you think. Silos in education mean that your teams are asked to implement so many practices and programs resulting in time becoming short for our teaching teams. Technology needs one group to learn a new learning management system. Research and Assessment needs another group to learn about formative assessment practices. Instructional Leadership has decided to implement another new curriculum for the third time in ten years. Your teachers and educational team members are asked to learn and integrate new information every year. Prioritizing this work when you know that you will hear complaints from many is a serious barrier to overcome.

And overcome you must, because without new models of relating to each other, to understand each other and to resolve challenges collaboratively, your school will not be ready for the future that is growing as we speak. As technology usage increases, research is already showing that children's expressive language skills emerge later than previously and that social skill development is changing. Technology, with all of its benefits, comes with a cost, one that the schools will bear responsibility to address. Teachers will need the help of their colleagues and to weather the emotional storms that are ahead for education. In the book, we have talked extensively about the needs of teachers and their perspective on education. Teachers feel disempowered and unsupported. The truth is, so do the other members of your instructional teams, from OTs and SLPs to instructional assistants and instructional coaches – the drumbeat of isolation and silo mentality is loud.

As the World Health Organization sought to inform global health challenges, this group came to recognize that no organization can do it alone. The world is dealing with emergencies of unprecedented scale. With 130 million people needing humanitarian assistance worldwide, the WHO identified interprofessional collaborative practice as a solution. In their Framework for Action on Interprofessional Education and Collaborative Practice, the WHO recommends focusing on the development of a "collaborative practice-ready" health workforce that is better prepared to respond to local health needs than current medical models. Training on this model is necessary in order to have competent collaborative practice-ready health workers. This idea started within the medical establishment, however, it is relevant to the dynamic needs of our education sector.

As you look to bring these shifts in mindset, you will face challenges.

1. There's not enough time to introduce a new method.

Your schedules are already filled, but you know that the Four Perspectives holds promise for your teams. You might be tempted to scale down the implementation plan and simply offer an overview. Of course, share these ideas freely, but if you want real change, you will need to invest time to make it happen. Research tells us that without a plan carried out by an implementation team, it will take seventeen years for 14 percent of your staff to be using the new innovation. With a plan and an implementation team, it will take three years for 80 percent of your staff to be using the new innovation. To get the biggest bang for your buck, you will need to find time and prioritize this learning. I provided ways you could schedule this for your staff in Chapter 8.

2. Teachers don't have time to work in teams.

Most teachers' experience with teams is pretty dismal. Initially, you will hear that more team-based work is a drain on the system. The truth is, you don't have time to not work in team-based models.

Teachers need to rely on each other and their expertise and knowledge to figure out ways to help students. Our job is to teach them how to work effectively within a team-based structure. They are right that when teams are ineffective, it's a waste of time. No teams should be operating without the knowledge of how to establish a high-performing team.

3. This is a special education problem, not a general education problem.

You will hear that this is something that special education needs to address and that it is a waste of time for the general education teacher. While many struggling students are students with disabilities, all of them are not. And regardless of whether the student is labeled special education or not, the reality is that greater than 65 percent of students with disabilities are educated within the general education classroom. The Four Perspectives simply clarifies the complexity of the problems teachers are seeking to solve and so this work will benefit all of your staff.

4. I don't know these concepts well enough to teach them.

This book provides an overview of the concepts and offers some suggestions for where additional information can be found. It is true, however, that as an administrator, you may have an intuitive understanding of these concepts but do not feel you could organize a professional development for your whole staff. You may decide that hiring a consultant, like me, is the right thing to do.

As a leader committed to helping teachers resolve challenges with struggling learners, I know how hard it is to move forward when the stress levels of your teams are high, when the cries are loud, and when the path forward seems laden with barriers. I take it one step at a time knowing that with each step, I am closer to the outcome I am pursuing. I have found that teams benefit from my persistence to the Four Perspectives. I know we can achieve more and so I operate through this lens without waver.

I want you to discover that there are answers to the concerns presented by struggling learners and that your teachers have the answers. Teachers just need you to give them the tools to understand how to solve problems in this difficult time in education history. Put them in teams, give them the tools to understand deeply the needs of the students they are supporting, and hold them accountable to using the strongest evidence-based practices. You will see. Things get better.

YOU CAN DO THIS!

Sir Ken Robinson, British author, speaker, and international advisor on education, said, "To improve our schools, we have to humanize them and make education personal to every student and teacher in the system. Education is always about relationships. Great teachers are not just instructors and test administrators: They are mentors, coaches, motivators, and lifelong sources of inspiration to their students." We can understand this cognitively, believe it's true, and still not know how to go about doing this. This has been the greatest lesson of my career. Change requires a desire to understand. Many teachers come to this naturally through an intrinsic curiosity about learning. Yet even for the most dedicated teacher, there may be situations that they cannot solve with the tools they have. How do we create change? How do we solve problems? Why do some teachers and instructional teams find success and others do not? In my experience, the number one factor is the understanding of the systems they work within and the perspectives through which they seek to find solutions.

Working with the variety of teachers and instructional team members in all levels and programs within my school system has shown me that there is no bad teacher and there are no bad kids. There are just people who are trying with the tools they have to do the job of school every day. We are not all equipped the same and so as we seek to provide more options for students by giving them skills for understanding, calculating, and relating, we must also acknowledge that as teachers and leaders, we too must develop new tools to do this work effectively.

The physicist Nassim Haramein has said that the universe is trying to understand itself through us. When I look out at the world through my eyes, I see it through the vantage point of my physical location and my personal experiences. But the world is not only what I can see or know. As another looks back at me, they too are looking at the world, but what they see and understand is different. Through these – different perspectives – we can come to know the whole. This wise perspective on a universal problem is exactly what we are doing when we help another. We see the other through our own eyes all while knowing that the other is not all that we can see in that moment.

It takes training and practice to allow the whole picture to be there – the good, the bad, the great, and the not so great. When we seek to help a student overcome a challenge, we must be willing to see the whole situation even when that means that we are or have created the problem we are trying to solve. At this time in world history, the best way to see the whole or to come as close as possible to seeing the whole is by inviting others to share their perspective and knowledge. Collaboration that is built to allow for high performance is not optional. What do they see about the child? What do they know about the child? Equally as important is the realization that our teachers and instructional teams need guidance in this time of change and social upheaval. We are all trying to understand the world and looking for how we can help make things better. Starting here, at school, is the best place to contribute to finding the solution the world is seeking. Here, we learn to value the differences in others because it is through the differences that we can see the whole more clearly.

The predictability of our lives can trick us into thinking a situation is simple, black or white. When we dedicate time and attention to learning to see beyond, the amount of potential and possibility that emerges is wondrous. The introduction to this work in Chapters 4 to 8 is just that, an introduction. You cannot really know this work until you begin to use it and learn from it.

We started this journey acknowledging that the world is watching as you navigate great social upheavals. How do we protect students and teachers and our communities as we learn to respect and value those who are different from us? How do we continue to grow to our potential in the midst of an international pandemic? How do we embrace the coming changes while stewarding a crew who is unclear, unprepared, and sometimes unwilling to travel the new course? Solutions are available to you, but not ones that can be found in a box. It is time for the teacher tool kit to expand. I've provided you with the Four Perspectives that I believe are needed in education and that many teachers do not have opportunities to learn in their preparation programs.

- Perspective 1: Effective Teams recognizes that all of teaching is collaborative, but few collaborations are highly effective. Teachers need tools to collaborate effectively and make teamwork beneficial.

- Perspective 2: Systems Thinking offers considerations that impact a student's response to a teaching strategy. When teachers understand the systems that a child exists within, we can tailor a more complete and responsive solution.

- Perspective 3: The Diverse Classroom illuminates the predictable make-up of a classroom with strengths and weaknesses across domains of development that can be anticipated and acted upon. In this domain, teachers also consider cultural responsiveness.

• Perspective 4: Evidence-Based Practice is the real powerhouse of the Four Perspectives. Teachers learn that not all practices are equal and discover that when they select the strongest practices, their impact on the child's success changes significantly.

I know you are a skilled principal and education leader who has tried everything to help. You wouldn't be reading this book if you weren't committed to your teachers and to helping them solve problems. However, if this is keeping you from devoting sufficient time to your administrative duties, something needs to change. I know that your teachers could solve some problems in the classroom on their own, resulting in more time for you to lead. And you know that if you do not solve this problem, your burnout is a real possibility. The Four Perspectives framework was developed to help your teachers find more success in solving student problems in the classroom. My hope is that you use this resource to help teachers learn to focus on what matters most when students struggle. When teachers look at foundational practices first and collaborate effectively with the many experts available to them, they will find success. Students will improve. Referrals will decrease. Whether you choose to lead your teachers on this journey on your own or to invite an experienced coordinator like me to help, I wish you the greatest success!

THANK YOU

I appreciate that you have taken the time to read my book. I know you recognize how important adding these skills to your teachers' instructional repertoire is. Seeing problems through the Four Perspectives is a process that your teachers and education teams can learn, and I want to support you as much as possible.